IASA-TITLE VI

MATT CHRISTOPHER

On the Mound with...
Greg Maddux

Little, Brown and Company
Boston   New York   Toronto   London

To Doris and Bill

First Edition

Cover photograph by Ronald C. Modra

Library of Congress Cataloging-in-Publication Data
Christopher, Matt.
    Greg Maddux / Matt Christopher.
       p.   cm.
    Summary: A biography of the Atlanta Braves' pitcher who has won the Cy Young Award four times and was named baseball's Player of the Year in 1995.
    ISBN 0-316-14191-7
    1. Maddux, Greg, 1966– —Juvenile literature.   2. Baseball play-ers—United   States—Biography—Juvenile   literature.   3.   Atlanta Braves (Baseball   team)—Juvenile   literature.   [1.   Maddux,   Greg, 1966– .   2.   Baseball players.]   I. Title.
GV865.M233C57   1997
796.357'092 — dc20
[B]   96–40973

10 9 8 7 6 5 4 3 2

MV-NY

Published simultaneously in Canada
by Little, Brown & Company (Canada) Limited

Printed in the United States of America

Contents

Chapter One

The Best Pitcher in Baseball

Greg Maddux doesn't look like the best pitcher in baseball. But he is. In 1992, 1993, 1994, and 1995, Greg won the National League's Cy Young Award. Named after Cy Young, baseball's all-time victory leader with 511 career wins, the award is given each year to the best pitcher in each major league. No other pitcher has ever won the award four years in a row.

In his ten-year big league career (through 1995), Greg has won 150 games and lost only 93. In his four Cy Young seasons, he won 75 games, and lost only 19.

Still, if you didn't know better, you'd never guess that Greg Maddux is such a great pitcher. Although Greg is more than thirty years old, he looks like he just got out of high school. For a professional athlete, he isn't very big. Greg stands only six feet tall and he weighs only 175 pounds. Off the baseball field, Greg wears glasses and dresses like someone in college. If he walked into your school today, you might think he was a student teacher dropping in to observe a class.

Even when Greg is wearing a baseball uniform and warming up before a game, he still doesn't look like the best pitcher in baseball. Greg is small for a pitcher, and he doesn't throw the ball as hard as most big league hurlers do, either. Most major league pitchers throw at least 90 miles an hour. Randy Johnson and Roger Clemens regularly throw the ball over 95 miles per hour, so fast that the hitter can barely tell where the ball is going before it smacks into the catcher's mitt.

Although Greg was once able to throw 90 miles an hour, he doesn't throw that hard anymore. He rarely throws a ball faster than about 85 miles per hour. That's still fast, but it's not fast for the major leagues. There is probably someone on your local high school team who throws close to 85 miles per hour.

Of course, Greg throws more than a fastball. He

also throws a "cut fastball," or "cutter," that moves, a curveball, and a change-up. But none of these pitches is much better than those thrown by many other players. If you watched all the pitchers on Greg's team, the Atlanta Braves, warm up before a game, and then you had to guess who was best, Greg Maddux would probably be the last guy you would pick!

Even when Greg takes the mound during a game, he doesn't look like the best pitcher in baseball. He doesn't strike out very many hitters. In fact, he doesn't even want to strike out most hitters. Most batters facing Greg eventually hit the ball, and that's fine with him. The best pitcher in baseball actually wants the batter to hit the ball!

So when does Greg Maddux look like the best pitcher in baseball? At the end of the game. That's when his teammates run out to the mound to congratulate him on another victory, while the hitters on the opposing team sit in the dugout dejectedly shaking their heads, wondering why they only managed to collect five or six hits and scored only one or two runs.

How does Greg Maddux do it? What makes him the best pitcher in the major leagues?

Greg is the perfect example of someone who just tries to do the very best he can with the talent he has. Since he doesn't have a great fastball, Greg learned that to be successful he had to do more than throw the ball by the hitter. He pitches with his brains as much as he does with his arm. Greg simply outthinks most hitters.

Imagine that you are at the plate and Greg Maddux is on the mound. You've watched him warm up and you feel confident. After all, he doesn't throw the ball as fast as most pitchers, and everyone knows you're a good hitter.

Greg looks in at his catcher, winds up slowly, and throws his first pitch.

It's a fastball, just what you were hoping for!

The ball looks like it's going to go right over the middle of the plate, so you decide to swing. But at the last second, the ball tails away and darts to the outside corner.

Oh no, you think to yourself, that's not just a fastball! It's Greg's cutter, a pitch thrown almost as hard as a fastball that curves a little bit at the last second. But it's too late to stop your swing. Instead of hitting the ball squarely, you foul it off for strike one.

Okay, you think, since I fouled that ball off, he probably doesn't think I can hit the ball low and out-side. This time, I'll be ready.

Greg goes into his windup, and you're expecting another pitch in the same place.

Wrong! This time Greg throws you a change-up, a pitch that looks like a fastball at first but is about 20 miles per hour slower. The pitch is waist high, on the inside part of the plate, just where you like it. But you are expecting a fastball outside and swing before the ball even gets to the plate. You miss it by a foot. Strike two!

Now you're really confused. You don't know what Greg will throw next. But Greg does.

He winds up and pitches. The rapidly spinning ball sails to the outside then curves away. You are so confused that you don't even bother swinging. But you get lucky. The pitch is just an inch or two outside, and the umpire calls it a ball.

Now what do you do? Where will Greg throw the next pitch? What pitch will he use? How fast will he throw it? Will it be inside or outside, high or low? Will he throw a fastball, a curve, or something else?

Greg winds up again and throws.

A fastball! But it's not where you expected him to throw it. You were looking to the outside part of the plate. Wrong again! This time Greg threw the ball inside, an inch or two below your belt. Normally, you'd smack an 85-mile-per-hour fastball like that over the fence for a home run. But Greg fooled you by throwing it inside. You swing anyway, but you don't get your bat around fast enough. You hit the ball off the handle.

The ball slowly dribbles out toward the mound. Greg fields it cleanly and flips it to the first baseman as you race down the line. You're out by twenty feet.

As you turn and jog back to the dugout, you ask yourself, "How did I miss that pitch?"

You missed it because Greg Maddux is the best pitcher in baseball, that's why. But don't feel too bad. You have plenty of company. Nearly every batter in the National League has asked himself the same question.

Chapter Two
1966–1976

Learning to Play the Game

It may be hard to believe, but Greg Maddux's pitching career began on a softball field.

Dave Maddux, Greg's father, was a member of the United States Air Force. He and his wife, Linda, Greg's mother, traveled all over the world as Dave was transferred from one air force base to another.

Dave Maddux loved sports, particularly baseball. But there wasn't an opportunity to play baseball on base. The air force only sponsored softball leagues. So no matter where Dave Maddux was stationed, the first thing he did was join the air force–base softball team.

Dave didn't play slo-pitch softball. That's the kind of softball that is often played in local parks on Saturday morning. In slo-pitch, the pitcher tosses the ball underhand toward the plate, and it is easy for hitters to hit.

Dave played fast-pitch softball, a game more similar to baseball than other kinds of softball.

In fast-pitch softball, the pitcher stands only fifty feet away from the batter. Instead of throwing the ball overhand, as in baseball, or lofting it underhand, as in other kinds of softball, in fast-pitch softball, the pitcher winds up like a windmill and throws the ball underhand as fast as he can. The ball travels almost as fast as a baseball, and despite its larger size, it can be just as hard to hit. Games are often low scoring.

Dave Maddux was a pitcher. He liked the fact that a fast-pitch softball pitcher could use the same strategy as a baseball pitcher. He could throw so fast that the hitter couldn't catch up to the ball, make it curve so it would be hard to hit, or change speeds and move the ball around the plate to upset the hitter's timing.

Dave Maddux was a good pitcher. He didn't just throw fast. He also tried to upset the batter's timing.

In 1959, the young couple had their first child, a

daughter they named Terri. Two years later, while stationed in Dayton, Ohio, Linda Maddux gave birth to a son, Mike.

Mike loved watching his father play ball. As soon as Mike could walk, Dave Maddux began teaching his son how to play. When he got off duty at three-thirty in the afternoon, Dave took Mike into the backyard and played baseball. He taught Mike how to throw, how to bat, how to field, and how to pitch.

After Dave was transferred to an air force base in San Angelo, Texas, Linda gave birth to another son. Gregory Alan Maddux was born on April 14, 1966.

Like his father and older brother, Greg learned to love baseball. As soon as he was old enough, he joined Mike and his father in the backyard.

Dave had fun with his sons, but he was serious about the way he taught them to play baseball. He made sure they learned to play the right way. Before the boys were old enough to attend school, Dave had taught them how to play sound, fundamental baseball. Mike and Greg learned how to field ground balls correctly and how to throw accurately. Their father taught them how to swing

9

level and to run hard down the first base line every time.

Even though Greg was four and a half years younger than his brother, in their backyard games, Dave Maddux tried to treat the boys equally. While Mike was bigger and a better player, Greg always tried to keep up with his brother.

The two boys had a great time growing up. When their father was on duty, they had each other, and there were always plenty of other kids to play with on the air force base. Even when the air force transferred Dave to Spain, his two sons had no trouble finding other boys to play baseball.

While the family lived in Spain, Greg acquired a nickname. One day at school, Greg copied out a work sheet in Spanish class. At the top of the sample work sheet was the fictitious name Nate Yates. Greg copied the name onto his own work sheet and brought the assignment home. His parents laughed at his error and started calling Greg Nate. Even today, they still sometimes refer to Greg as Nate. If you hear someone calling Greg that from the stands at a game, it may be Greg's parents!

No matter where Mike went, Greg tagged along. He worshiped his older brother and wanted to become a good baseball player just like him.

When Mike joined his friends at the base park to play baseball, he brought Greg. At first, the other kids looked at Greg and asked Mike, "Why did you have to bring him along? Greg's too little to play with us. He might get hurt."

Mike Maddux just laughed. He knew from their backyard practices that his little brother was already just as good, if not better, than most of his friends.

"You guys just watch," he said. "My little brother knows how to play baseball."

Mike was right. Despite his small size, Greg was able to keep up with boys three and four years older than he was.

Soon Greg was being picked ahead of most of the older boys when the group chose sides for games. When he became old enough to play Little League, he was so good that in his first season he played against boys two or three years older.

Both Maddux boys were stars in Spain's Little League. But, although they enjoyed Little League, they had even more fun playing whiffle ball against each other in the backyard.

A whiffle ball is a hollow plastic baseball with holes cut in it that cause the ball to swerve or dip when it is thrown. Because the ball is plastic, it is difficult to hit it very far, and it is very safe to use. Whiffle balls don't break windows, so they are great to play with in the backyard.

The two boys made up their own game. Each would pitch against the other. Where and how far the ball was hit determined whether or not it was an out, a double, or a home run.

Like their father, the Maddux boys were big Cincinnati Reds fans. In the early 1970s, the Cincinnati Reds were one of the most powerful teams in baseball. Their lineup included players like Pete Rose, the all-time major league leader in hits; Hall of Fame catcher Johnny Bench; and speedy second baseman Joe Morgan, also a Hall of Famer.

While at bat, each boy would imitate a hitter in the Reds lineup, often announcing each play like a radio broadcaster.

Greg's favorite player was Pete Rose. He'd crouch in the imaginary batter's box as Mike wound up and threw.

"Here's Pete Rose," Greg would announce, "looking for his first hit of the game. Here's the pitch . . ."

Crack! Greg would swing and smack the ball past his brother, then each boy would turn to the other and laugh. They played the game for hours almost every day. They were having fun, but they were also learning to be better baseball players. Hitting against the swerving whiffle ball was good batting practice, and deciding what pitch to throw was good practice for becoming a pitcher.

When Mike was fourteen and Greg was ten, Dave Maddux was transferred back to the United States, to an air force base near Las Vegas, Nevada.

When most people hear the name Las Vegas, they think of the big gambling casinos that light up the downtown district and the famous entertainers who put on shows there. But Las Vegas is more than a city of slot machines. It has fine schools, and because of the warm desert weather, baseball can be played there nearly all year.

13

That was perfect for the Maddux brothers. There was nothing they liked to do more than play baseball. And it was in this city that the Maddux family met a man who would help both boys further their baseball careers.

Chapter Three
1976-1984

"Don't Let Anybody Change Him"

Rusty Medar was a retired major league scout who scoured Las Vegas looking for promising young ballplayers. He invited hot prospects to attend informal Sunday afternoon practice sessions. He liked helping young players. Shortly after the Madduxes moved to Las Vegas, Medar heard that Mike Maddux was a really good player and invited him to attend the sessions.

Mike's father and Greg tagged along. After several weeks, Dave Maddux approached Medar and asked, "Why don't you let Greg play?"

Medar looked at the scrawny eleven-year-old and reluctantly agreed. He was just being nice. He didn't think Greg would be able to keep up with the older boys.

But the first time Medar saw Greg throw, his reluctance turned to enthusiasm. He watched as Greg wound up and threw the ball to another boy. Greg's pitching motion was smooth. He wound up and released the ball the exact same way each time. He was completely balanced and looked totally at ease.

"Mr. Maddux," said Medar, "I don't know where the boy got those mechanics, but let me tell you. Don't let anybody change him."

Medar was referring to Greg's windup. Pro players and coaches refer to the particulars of a pitcher's windup as his "mechanics." They know that if a pitcher has good mechanics, he has a good chance of throwing a pitch where he wants to.

Most pitchers play for years before they learn how to throw correctly. But Greg already knew how. All those backyard practices with his father and hours spent playing whiffle ball with Mike had paid off.

Greg kept attending Medar's practices with Mike. In the winter, college players and local professionals sometimes showed up at the park to keep in shape. For years, Greg was the youngest boy there. But he wasn't intimidated. He had always played against older players.

Medar worked closely with him. He wanted Greg

to realize that there was a lot more to pitching than just rearing back and throwing the ball as hard as you can.

While many of Greg's peers were getting sore arms from throwing curveballs incorrectly, Medar taught Greg how to throw a change-up.

"Throwing a curveball now can hurt your arm," Medar told him. "Besides, a good change-up is the hardest pitch in the world to hit."

When Greg pitched, Medar often stood behind him, telling him exactly what to do. He didn't just tell Greg to throw strikes. In fact, he sometimes told him to throw balls!

"That's where I started to learn about pitching," Greg told a reporter years later. "I started to understand some of the theories of pitching."

Medar taught Greg that control is a pitcher's best weapon. Control is not just the ability to throw strikes but the ability to throw a pitch precisely where you want to in order to set the batter up for another pitch. That's why Medar sometimes asked Greg to throw pitches out of the strike zone.

Greg wasn't the only Maddux who was getting better. Mike was a star pitcher in high school. After his senior year, he was drafted by the Cincinnati Reds.

Despite the fact that Mike had been drafted by the Reds, his favorite team, he decided to accept a scholarship to the University of Texas at El Paso instead. Neither Medar nor Dave Maddux thought Mike was quite ready for professional baseball. They believed that a few years of college baseball would help Mike to mature and grow stronger.

While Mike was away at college, Greg continued to improve. But baseball wasn't his whole life. He was a normal teenager. In the summer, Greg worked part time making hamburgers at Wendy's restaurant. In the fall and winter, he played a lot of basketball.

When Greg began high school, Mike Maddux sat down with him and gave him some advice.

"If I were you," he said, "I'd forget basketball. Your future is in baseball, and you should concentrate on that."

Greg agreed. Mike had told him how hard he had to work at baseball in college and how good the players were. Greg knew that if he ever hoped to play in college or professionally he would have to be totally dedicated to pitching.

Greg was fortunate enough to attend Valley High School. Under coach Roger Fairless, Valley had one of the best high school baseball programs in the country. A number of Valley alumni had gone on to professional baseball careers. One player, pitcher Mike Morgan, had been selected in the first round of the baseball draft in 1978 by the Oakland A's.

At first, Greg was a good player at Valley, but he wasn't a star. He didn't play very much as a sophomore. In his junior year, Valley won the state championship. Greg hit a grand slam home run in the championship game and was named to the All-State team, though back trouble had kept him from pitching as much as he wanted to that season.

Meanwhile, it seemed as if everyone Greg knew was getting a chance to play pro baseball. Brother Mike was drafted out of college by the Philadelphia Phillies. This time, Mike Maddux signed. And dozens of scouts were turning out at Valley games to watch Greg's teammate, Mike Greer, pitch.

In one game, Greer, who was eventually drafted and signed by the Cleveland Indians, was replaced by Greg. Chicago Cubs scout Ray Handley, in the stands to watch Greer, discovered he liked the little junior right-hander named Maddux. He told local scout Doug Mapson to keep an eye on him.

Mike Maddux was pitching his way through the minor leagues while Greg was still in high school. When his brother called or when he returned home in the winter, Greg couldn't wait to talk with him.

Mike gave Greg more than good advice on how to pitch. He warned him that if he ever got a chance to play professionally, he had to take it seriously.

"There are a lot of players who screw up and never get out of the minors," he told Greg. "It's amazing how much talent is wasted."

Greg worked hard. By the end of his senior year, it was obvious that he had the talent to play pro ball. Although he threw only in the mid-80s, he was still way too fast for most high school hitters, and Greg had much more control and poise than most pitchers his age. When he didn't pitch, he played center field and was one of the best hitters on the team.

Greg's high school coach, Roger Fairless, remembers Greg well. As he told a reporter several years later, "The thing that always made Greg different was his control and poise on the mound. He just never got behind or into trouble."

Except once.

Coach Fairless usually called each pitch from the bench. Late in his senior year, Greg convinced Fairless to let him call his own game. Greg quickly learned that he didn't know quite as much about pitching as he thought. In the first inning, a batter hit a home run. Greg started trying too hard, and the game turned into a rout. Greg lost, 8–0.

But that wasn't enough to discourage interest in him. At every game he pitched, there were more and more professional scouts. It seemed likely that he would follow in his brother's footsteps and be drafted right out of high school. The scouts were worried about just one thing: Greg's size.

Greg was five feet eleven inches tall and weighed only 145 pounds. Major league scouts worried that he wouldn't have enough stamina to pitch well for very long. Had Greg been only a few inches taller and weighed 200 pounds, he would have been one of the first picks in the draft. But scouts told Dave Maddux that because of Greg's size, he might not be picked until the second or third round.

Size was not the most pressing issue on Greg's mind, however. Like his brother, Mike, before him, he had a decision to make. He had already been of-fered a scholarship to play baseball for the University of Arizona. UA had one of the best collegiate baseball programs in the country. Many alumni had gone on to successful careers in pro baseball. Greg was going to have to choose between turning pro immediately and attending college.

June 4, 1984, was draft day. Greg was in Hawaii on Valley High's class of 1984 senior trip. When he returned home, his parents told him he had been drafted.

The Chicago Cubs, using the third pick of the second round, had selected Greg. Overall, he was the thirty-first player in the entire country selected in the draft.

Greg was thrilled to be such a high draft pick. Doug Mapson, whom Greg had met many times as he was being scouted, went to the Maddux home to try to convince Greg to sign a contract.

The Cubs scout was honest with Greg and his family. "If you're just going to college to pitch," he told them, "you'd probably be better off signing with us now."

That made sense to Greg. The University of

Arizona had a deep, veteran pitching staff, and Greg knew it might take a year or two before he would be allowed to pitch very often. If he signed with the Cubs, he'd be able to pitch in the minors right away. Besides, Greg knew that if he started attending college, he would be ineligible for the professional draft for three years. And in three years, anything could happen.

The Cubs offered Greg an $85,000 bonus to turn pro. To Greg, that seemed like all the money in the world.

It was enough, he decided, that if he didn't make it to the big leagues, he could still put himself through college. He promised his parents he wouldn't touch the bonus money until he made the major leagues. Dave and Linda Maddux agreed to let Greg turn professional.

The moment Greg signed his name to the contract, he became a professional baseball player.

Chapter Four
1984-1986

Minor Leagues and Major Changes

The Cubs had Greg report to their minor league team in Pikeville, North Carolina. Pikeville played in the Appalachian League, what professional baseball refers to as a "Single A," or "A" league.

Each major league team has what is called a "farm system," a group of minor league clubs that they use to give players experience before they reach the major leagues. The lowest minor leagues are called "rookie" leagues. Next are A, AA, and AAA; Triple A is only one step below the major leagues.

Most players who sign out of high school are assigned to a rookie league team. But the Cubs thought Greg was good enough to play A ball, so they sent him straight to Pikeville.

Minor league baseball is a big adjustment for most players. Not only is the competition better than it is in high school or college, but players must adjust to living on their own. Some young players become homesick and never play to their full potential. Others become undisciplined and waste time partying or getting into trouble.

For many of Greg's Pikeville teammates, it was the first time they ever lived away from home. Greg was more fortunate. Because his family had moved so often when he was growing up, he was used to adjusting to new places. And he had his brother. Mike Maddux had already told him what to expect in the minor leagues. Greg had heard Mike tell stories about the long bus rides from town to town and how difficult it was living in cheap motels while on road trips. Mike cautioned Greg to stay focused on what he wanted to accomplish, which was reaching the big leagues.

Greg still had to make adjustments. Everyone in the minors had been a star in high school or college. In every game Greg pitched, he faced hitters who were better than any he had ever pitched against before.

But Greg did have one advantage. In professional baseball, hitters use wooden bats instead of the aluminum ones used in most high schools and colleges. It is easier to hit with an aluminum bat. The ball comes off an aluminum bat a little faster and goes farther than it does off a wooden one. Also, when a hitter gets jammed by a pitch and hits it off the handle of a wooden bat, the bat usually breaks, and the ball rolls weakly away. If he hits a pitch on the handle of an aluminum bat, it might end up as a line drive base hit. Many good hitters in high school and college never make the adjustment to a wooden bat in pro ball.

That helped Greg. If he could make good pitches, it would actually be harder for a hitter to get a base hit with a wooden bat. Greg knew he would have to make use of any small edge he could get in order to succeed.

Greg pitched well in Pikeville. His control was better than that of most pitchers in the league, and his fastball was quick enough to get by most hitters. In fourteen appearances for Pikeville, Greg was 6–2, including two shutouts. His 2.63 earned run average, or ERA, was fifth best in the league.

Earned run average is one of the most important pitching statistics. It measures the average number of runs a pitcher gives up for every nine innings pitched, not counting runs that score because of errors. A 3.00 ERA means a pitcher gives up an average of three runs every nine innings. An ERA of 3.00 or below is considered very good.

Greg's first-year performance earmarked him as a future star. In the off-season, the Cubs sent him to the Arizona Instructional League.

As the name suggests, the instructional league is designed to help players learn new skills. Winning is not as important as it is in a regular-season league. Players are able to practice a new position, learn a new pitch, try a new batting stance, or just gain extra experience.

Usually, only the best minor league prospects are sent to the instructional league. Greg was tested by hitters much more skilled than those he had faced in the Appalachian League. But Greg pitched even better in Arizona than he had in Pikeville. The better the hitters were, the better he seemed to pitch. In twenty-nine innings of work in Arizona, Greg's ERA was only 1.88.

In the spring, Greg was promoted to Peoria, Illinois, in the Midwest League. Although the

Midwest League was still an A league, it was considered to be better than the Appalachian League. Players were a year or two older and had already proven themselves in rookie leagues or A ball. Besides, Peoria was less than two hundred miles from Chicago. It was easy for the Cubs to keep track of Greg's progress.

Greg gave the Cubs plenty to keep track of, and by the end of the season he had proved he was more than ready to move on to the next level. He started twenty-seven ball games and ended up pitching almost 200 innings. He won thirteen games and had one of the lowest ERAs in the league. Even though Greg was only nineteen years old, Cubs fans were starting to keep track of his performance.

But the Cubs didn't want to rush Greg. They thought Greg could be a star and they didn't want to ruin his confidence by sending him to the big leagues before he was ready. Since Greg was so young, the Cubs decided to be patient with him.

They chose to move Greg up through the minor leagues one step at a time. In the spring of 1986, the Cubs sent Greg to their team in Pittsfield, Massachusetts, in the AA Eastern League.

As young pitchers rise through the minor league levels, many begin to question their abilities. Often, when they move from one level to the next, they try to change the way they pitch. Just as often, they fail and have a difficult time rediscovering exactly what made them successful.

That didn't happen to Greg Maddux. At each stop on the minor league ladder, he just kept pitching the way he always had. He didn't try to strike everyone out. He just tried to throw strikes and keep the hitters off balance by changing the speed of his pitches. Greg's style was just as effective in Pittsfield as it had been in Arizona, Peoria, and Pikeville. In his first eight starts, he went 4–3, including two shutouts, with an ERA of only 2.69.

That was enough for the Cubs. They promoted Greg to their AAA farm team at Iowa in the American Association.

Pitching at AAA was Greg's final test, the last step before the big leagues. In AAA, most players have a lot of experience. Many have played five or six years in the minor leagues, and some have even played in the major leagues. If Greg could get hitters out with Iowa, his next stop would be Wrigley Field in Chicago. The major leagues.

Once again, Greg just kept pitching the only way he knew. The same strategies that had worked for him in A and AA worked in Iowa, too. In eighteen starts, Greg won ten games and lost only one. He threw two shutouts, and his ERA was just over 3.00. As he gained experience, Greg pitched even better. In August, he was undefeated, and his ERA was a stellar 1.60.

His performance got the Cubs' attention. Iowa's season ended at the beginning of September. For most minor leaguers, that marks the beginning of the off-season. But on September 1, major league teams are allowed to expand their rosters from the usual twenty-four players to forty. This allows them to see how well younger players will perform in the major leagues.

After winning the Eastern Division of the National League in 1984, the Cubs had slumped and finished in fourth place in 1985. In 1986, they were even worse. Entering September, Chicago was in fifth place, more than thirty games behind the first-place New York Mets.

With no championship at stake, on September 1, 1986, the Cubs called up nearly a dozen minor league players. One of those was Greg Maddux.

Greg was thrilled. A few months before, his brother, Mike, had been recalled by the Philadelphia Phillies. Both brothers were now in the major leagues.

They had come a long way. Only a few years before, they had been playing whiffle ball in the backyard and dreaming about playing against each other in the major leagues. Now, that dream was about to come true.

Chapter Five
1986

Big League Brothers

Greg joined the Cubs in Chicago. After checking into a hotel, he made his way to Wrigley Field.

Wrigley Field is one of the oldest and most beautiful ballparks in the major leagues. Like many old ballparks, it is small, and the outfield fence has all sorts of quirky angles. The Wrigley Field fence is made of brick and covered with ivy. When Greg joined the team, Wrigley Field was the only park in major league baseball without lights. The Cubs played every home game during the day.

Cubs fans loved their old park and they loved the Cubs. But they hadn't had much to cheer about in a long, long time. The Cubs hadn't been to the World Series since 1945. They last won the series in 1908!

Making his debut with a second division team at

the end of the season was a good situation for Greg. There wasn't much pressure on him to do well. The Cubs could afford to let Greg pitch and not worry too much about winning or losing.

Greg didn't have to wait long to make his major league debut. On September 3, 1986, the Cubs were locked in a tie with the Houston Astros. Inning after inning went by, and the score remained tied. Then, in the eighteenth inning, the Cubs put Greg Maddux into the game.

It didn't stay tied for long after that. Greg gave up a long home run, and the Cubs lost. Greg was the losing pitcher.

Still, the Cubs gave Greg another chance. Four days later, on September 7 in Cincinnati, the Cubs selected Greg to be their starting pitcher against the Reds.

Greg could hardly believe it. As a child, he had played countless games of whiffle ball pretending he was either playing for the Reds or pitching against them. Now, he was doing the real thing.

Fortunately for Greg, the 1986 Reds weren't quite the powerful "Big Red Machine" Greg had cheered for in the early 1970s. Still, they had a formidable lineup, led by sluggers Dave Parker, Nick Esasky, and Eric Davis. And pitching for the Reds was Bill Gullickson, who had already won thirteen games. It wouldn't be easy beating the Reds.

As Greg warmed up before the game, he was nervous but confident. He tried to tell himself to just keep pitching the way he had in the minor leagues.

In the first inning, the Cubs' second hitter, Chico Walker, hit a home run. The Cubs went on to score twice more to take a 3–0 lead. As Greg walked out to the mound, he started to relax. It was easier pitching with 3–0 lead. He didn't have to worry about making a mistake.

Only twenty years old, Greg was one of the youngest players in the major leagues, and the youngest Cub to start a game in twenty years. But the Reds soon found out that despite Greg's youth, he pitched like a veteran.

In the first inning, he had a memorable confrontation with Cincinnati slugger Dave Parker. Parker hugged the plate, and Greg was determined to make him back off. He threw his first pitch under Parker's chin, and the big hitter was forced to duck away. He stood there, glaring at Greg as if to say he had no right to pitch him there. Then Parker dug back in, still hugging the plate.

Greg's next pitch was just as close to Parker, and this time Parker yelled something at Greg and tried to intimidate him. But Greg didn't back down. He yelled right back and motioned for Parker to get back into the batter's box. Although Parker later collected three hits in the game, Greg had earned his respect.

He held the Reds scoreless in the first inning, and the game entered the second with the Cubs still ahead, 3–0.

In the second inning, the Cubs scored three more runs. Greg even got to bat, although he didn't get a hit. Now Chicago led 6–0.

With a big lead, all Greg had to do was throw strikes. He didn't have to worry if he gave up a hit or two. Throwing strikes was what Greg did best. He was able to spot his fastball on the corners, change speeds, and keep the hitters off balance. Although he gave up a couple of hits, he again held the Reds scoreless.

In the third inning, the Cubs scored three runs again to take a commanding 9–0 lead. Greg tried not to get overconfident.

The score was still 9–0 when the Cubs came to bat in the fifth inning. Shortstop Shawon Dunston homered to put the Cubs up 10–0. Greg stepped to the plate, still looking for his first major league hit. Although pitchers aren't expected to hit very well, Greg was an exception. He liked hitting, and for a pitcher, he hit well.

Cincinnati pitcher Carl Willis wound up and threw. Greg liked what he saw. *Crack!* He smacked a sharp ground ball through the infield for his first hit.

The Cubs left Greg stranded on base, and as he took the mound in the bottom of the fifth, he knew he just had to get out of the inning to become eligible for his first major league win. Starting pitchers must pitch five full innings to get credit for a victory.

The top of the order was up for Cincinnati. But the Reds decided to pinch hit for shortstop Kurt Stillwell. The announcer called out, "Now batting for Cincinnati, Dave Concepcion."

Greg couldn't believe it. Concepcion was the only player left on the Reds who had played for the team when Greg was a boy. Now he was pitching against him in the major leagues!

Greg was good for a young player, but the veteran Concepcion had seen it all. He would be hard to fool.

Nevertheless, Greg fooled him. Instead of a monster smash, Concepcion hit a slow ground ball to the left side. The Cubs' infielder got to the ball and threw to first, but Concepcion beat the throw for an infield hit. He moved to second on a ground out. Up stepped Dave Parker to the plate.

Greg had to be extra careful with Parker. If he made a mistake, Parker could hit a home run. Greg had to keep him in the ballpark.

He did, and although Parker's single plated Concepcion with the Reds' first run, Greg prevented him from hitting a home run and giving the Reds a big inning.

Greg was in command for the rest of the game. While the Reds kept nicking him for hits, and catcher Bo Diaz even cracked a home run off him in the sixth inning, Greg kept throwing tough pitches with men on base and worked himself out of several jams. The game ended 11–3. The Cubs had won, and although Greg had given up eleven hits and walked three batters, he had pitched the whole game and earned his first major league win.

Greg was excited after the game, but the sports-writers who crowded around his locker couldn't help but notice that he appeared calm. As Greg told them, "I'm kind of awestruck right now. Some of these guys I remember watching when I was ten years old."

After the game, Greg's minor league pitching coach, Jim Colburn, who had joined the Cubs coaching staff for the last month of the season, spoke to the reporters about Greg.

"He's a good competitor and fun to watch," said Colburn. "Especially knowing he just finished his paper route a couple of years ago."

When a reporter mentioned that it didn't seem as if Greg threw very hard, Colburn nodded his head in agreement. "I don't think it's fair to expect Greg to lead the league in strikeouts," he said. "He's not a strikeout pitcher and he probably won't ever win twenty-five or thirty games in the big leagues. But he should have a good big league career."

Colburn's words appeared to be optimistic after Greg's next few appearances. In each of his next three starts, he was hit hard. He lost all three. In another year, the Cubs might have given up on

Greg. But they weren't going to finish anywhere but in fifth place in 1986. The final week of the season, they decided to give Greg one more start.

Their opponents, the Philadelphia Phillies, weren't going anywhere either. Although the Phillies were in second place, the first-place Mets had clinched the division championship weeks before and led the Phillies by more than twenty games.

The day before the game, Greg checked to see who would be pitching for the Phillies. He couldn't believe it. Scheduled to pitch for the Phillies was Greg's brother, Mike!

Dave and Linda Maddux were unable to go to Philadelphia for the game, but they watched it on television. They enjoyed seeing both of their sons play, but to see them pitch against each other was a special treat. Still, it put them in an awkward position. Who would they root for?

They knew that although one of their sons would win and one would lose, they had to root for both. They just hoped that each son pitched well. Before the game, they called them and wished them luck.

Both Greg and Mike tried to act as if it were just another game, but they couldn't help thinking back to all those games of whiffle ball in the backyard. Each brother wanted to win badly.

The Cubs batted first. Chico Walker singled, then stole second and scored on a double by Ryne Sandberg. Cubs outfielder Keith Moreland, an extremely slow runner, hit an apparent single to right field, but Phillies right fielder Glenn Wilson charged the ball and threw to first.

"Out!" The first base umpire threw his thumb into the air. Moreland was thrown out at first on a ball hit to the outfield!

But while the Phillies were throwing Moreland out, Sandberg scored. Chicago and Greg Maddux led Philadelphia and Mike Maddux, 2–0.

Greg easily retired the Phillies in the first inning. Then the brothers settled into a pitching duel. Each had the opportunity to bat against the other, but neither collected a base hit. In the top of the fourth, the Cubs still led, 2–0.

Then Mike Maddux accidentally hit the first Cubs batter with a pitch. He gave up a single on the next batter. When the third man also singled, the Cubs led, 3–0, and Mike Maddux was lifted from the game.

When he got to the dugout, he took off his glove and slammed it against the wall. He didn't want to leave the game. He wanted to beat Greg.

But Greg wasn't about to be beaten. The Cubs scored three more runs to take a 6–0 lead in the fifth before Philadelphia was able to push across a run. Greg was pitching just as he had a few weeks before against Cincinnati. He was giving up hits, but not very many runs.

The final score was Chicago 8, Philadelphia 3. Greg gave up all three runs and ten hits in seven and two thirds innings to collect his second big league win. Mike was charged with six hits and three runs in three innings, and his record fell to 3–7.

After the game, Mike was as disappointed as Greg was happy. "Because he's my brother, I wanted to pitch well," said Mike. "But it will happen again, and next time I'll get him. This is not the first time he's beaten me. I think our record is .500 in backyard whiffle ball."

In the visitors' locker room, Greg couldn't help but smile. Still, he said, "I would have liked to have seen Mike do better, but I'm just glad we won." Then he admitted, "I look forward to any game, but this one was a little more fun. I had more pride in this one — winter's bragging rights."

Neither brother pitched again before the season ended. Both returned home to Las Vegas for the winter, looking forward to their next meeting on the mound and happy have pitched in the big leagues. But they knew they would have to work even harder to stay there.

Chapter Six
1987–1988

Gaining Control

The Cubs were encouraged by the way Greg had pitched during the last month of the 1986 season. Although he had scuffled a little, he had kept his composure.

Greg was encouraged, too. While he hadn't pitched quite as well as he had hoped, he had learned a lot and was confident that he could be successful in the big leagues. He knew the key was concentration. In the minors, he could miss with a pitch or throw the wrong one and the batter usually still made an out. In the big leagues, mistakes were automatic base hits.

Because they had finished the season with a losing record in 1986, in 1987 the Cubs decided to rebuild and go with their younger players. Greg worked hard in spring training and was given every opportunity to earn a spot in the Cubs' starting rotation.

Under the tutelage of Cubs pitching coach Herm Starette, Greg pitched fairly well and finished spring training with an ERA less than 4.00. He wasn't great yet, but he was good enough to become the Cubs' fifth starter.

Starette thought Greg had good tools but needed to work on keeping the ball down. In three years of minor league baseball, Greg's fastball had improved, and he threw it more often. Now the pitch occasionally hit 90 miles per hour. That was fast enough to get out minor league hitters, but Greg's fastball was straight. Unless the pitch moved a lot, or was thrown to the perfect place, Starette knew that veteran big leaguers would hit it, especially the second or third game they faced Greg.

But it was Greg's behavior on the mound that really began to trouble the Cubs. Starting in spring training, Greg had begun to act up while pitching. When he made a bad pitch, he sometimes screamed an obscenity at himself. He often argued with umpires and had a habit of pointing at hitters and telling them off in the middle of the game. Greg may have looked like a choirboy, but he was acting like a madman. His veteran teammates nicknamed him Mad Dog.

Such behavior, while not recommended for any pitcher, was especially troubling in a twenty-year-old rookie like Greg, the youngest player in the big leagues. It made the opposition even more determined to beat him and sometimes led umpires to call close pitches against him. Simply put, Greg was immature, and it showed.

Greg started the season in the Cubs' rotation and pitched well at first. On May 15, he picked up his third win of the young season by pitching his best game in the big leagues so far, holding Houston to only three hits in seven and two thirds innings to win, 3–1. The victory put the Cubs six games above .500 for the first time in two years. All of a sudden, people started thinking that Greg Maddux was going to be a star.

But as Greg became more successful, he began to get a little cocky. While he still listened to Coach Starette, when he took the mound, he sometimes pitched as if he wasn't paying any attention at all. When Greg got into a jam, he became afraid to throw his change-up and began throwing only fastballs, trying to throw each pitch faster than the one before. But the harder he threw, the harder it was for him to control exactly where the pitch was going. Before long, he was just throwing the ball down the middle of the plate — and hitters were starting to tee off.

San Diego outfielder Tony Gwynn later commented to a reporter about Greg Maddux, "What I saw back then was a guy who wasn't in control of himself. I remember thinking, unless he changes, he'll never control his pitching, either."

At first, the Cubs hoped that Greg was just in a slump and that sooner or later he would pitch his way out of it. But Greg became locked in a cycle of pitching poorly, getting angry, and throwing fastballs right down the middle. It was a cycle that had to be broken if he was to continue in the starting rotation.

By August, Greg's record was a dismal 6–10, and his ERA was 4.91. In desperation, the Cubs sent him back down to the minor leagues.

The move didn't surprise Greg or make him unhappy. In fact, he was relieved. He knew he wasn't pitching well and had expected to be sent down weeks before. As Greg later admitted, "I didn't really understand anything about pitching back then, didn't really understand anything about acting like a pitcher."

At AAA Iowa, Greg was reunited with Dick Pole, who had been his pitching coach in his first few minor league seasons. When Pole talked, Greg listened.

Pole made a few changes in the way Greg held the ball and stepped toward the plate during his delivery. When Greg took the mound for Iowa, he was a different pitcher. He made four starts and was magnificent, winning three games and allowing only three earned runs. Within two weeks, he was back with the Cubs.

But as quickly as Greg had turned his season around, he was right back where he had started. He was pummeled in his first start with the Cubs, and before the game ended was back pitching the way he had earlier in the year. By the end of the season, he had lost four more games, and his ERA had soared to nearly six runs per game.

Greg knew he had to do something drastic, and so did the Cubs. They were afraid that their best pitching prospect was quickly turning into a bust. Instead of waiting for spring training to begin preparing for the 1988 season, the Cubs asked Greg to play winter ball. He readily agreed.

When it is winter in the United States, the weather

is still warm in Latin America and the Caribbean. Winter Leagues in Puerto Rico, the Dominican Republic, and Venezuela operate to give many major and minor league ballplayers from Latin America an opportunity to play in front of their home fans.

Each season, some American minor leaguers and a few major leaguers also take advantage of the opportunity to play winter ball. As in the minors instructional league, players use the short winter season to develop skills they ordinarily couldn't in the major leagues. Some learn another position, while others simply try to improve.

Pitching coach Pole accompanied Greg to Venezuela, where he and Greg started from scratch. They decided to make a new Greg Maddux.

They changed almost everything about Greg's pitching, from the way he held the ball in his glove when he wound up to the way he gripped each pitch. While most of these changes would be barely noticeable to the average fan, they made a big difference in Greg's pitching. Now, nearly every pitch he threw moved. Hitters could no longer just sit back and wait for him to throw a straight fastball over the middle of the plate. When Greg aimed for the middle, the ball either curved or tailed away to the corner.

But the biggest change they made didn't have anything to do with Greg's mechanics. Pole worked with him on his approach to pitching. He tried to get Greg to understand that with every batter, in every situation, he had to pitch with a plan. It did no good just to try to throw the ball past every hitter. By intelligently choosing each pitch, and changing speeds, Greg would be able to set hitters up, to get them to expect one pitch and then be surprised by something else.

In each game Greg pitched in Venezuela, Pole insisted that he throw at least thirty change-ups. Coach Pole knew that if Greg did that, he would learn to throw the change-up for strikes and gain confidence in it. Then, when he was back pitching in the big leagues, Greg wouldn't be afraid to throw the pitch when he needed it.

But Greg didn't spend all his time in Venezuela thinking about pitching. He missed his girlfriend. In the middle of the winter season, between starts, he returned to the United States and married his high school sweetheart, Kathy. Then it was back to pitching again.

Pitching in the Winter League paid off. By throwing so many change-ups, Greg gained control of the pitch and began to learn how to outthink batters. At the end of the winter season, Greg was one of the best pitchers in the league.

Greg looked forward to the beginning of spring training. He became even more excited when he learned that Dick Pole would serve as the Cubs' pitching coach.

When Greg arrived at spring training in late February of 1988, he picked up right where he had left off in Venezuela. No longer dependent on the fastball, he impressed everyone, both with the way he pitched and the way he behaved. Now when Greg was on the mound, he was all business.

He received his first start of the regular season on April 6, against the Atlanta Braves. Although he struggled a little with his control and walked six batters, Greg gave up only three hits and shut out the Braves, 3–0.

After the game, Greg gave all the credit to Dick

Pole. "Last year, I just threw one fastball after another," he said. "Dick Pole can teach you a lot."

For the next few months, Greg had ample opportunity to show the rest of the National League exactly what he had learned. In his next start, he beat the St. Louis Cardinals, 6–1. By the end of May, he was 8–3 and had won four of his last five starts. All of a sudden, Greg was one of the best pitchers in baseball.

Greg did nothing to cause anyone to think otherwise. He just kept winning. By the end of June, he had won six more to improve his record to 14–3.

In early July, baseball's regular season stops for a few days so the American and National Leagues can play each other in the All-Star game. Fans all over America vote for the players they want to see in the game, except for pitchers. The managers of the All-Star teams get to select the pitchers.

Greg kept his fingers crossed. He wanted to make the All-Star team, but he didn't want to get his hopes too high. Two Cubs, outfielder Andre Dawson and second baseman Ryne Sandberg, had already been elected to the team. Since each league team must have at least one player on the squad, Greg knew that it might not be possible for him to be chosen, too.

A week before the game, Cardinals manager Whitey Herzog, the National League All-Star manager, named the pitchers. Greg had made the team!

He was ecstatic when he learned the news. "It's something I've never thought of before," he told a reporter. "How could I when I was 6–14 last year?"

Three days later, Greg celebrated his selection with his fifteenth victory of the year, beating the San Diego Padres, 4–2. He even knocked in the winning run with a single.

The All-Star game was two days later. Because he had just pitched, Greg didn't get to play in the 2–1 American League win. That was okay with him. He was just happy to be there.

Then, in the second half of the season, it was as if someone had flipped a switch. During the first half of the season, it had seemed as if Greg couldn't lose. But during the second half, it seemed he couldn't win.

In his first start after the All-Star game, Greg pitched well but didn't get a decision, as the game went into extra innings. Then he got belted in five innings and took the loss against San Francisco.

A few days later, the Cubs traveled to Philadelphia.

While Greg was fast becoming a superstar in Chicago, brother Mike was struggling with the Phillies. He had begun the year on the disabled list with a sore elbow before being activated on June 1. Since then, Mike Maddux had worked his way into the Phillies' starting rotation. Once again, the two Maddux brothers would face each other on the mound.

Everyone expected Greg to win the rematch. After all, he was 15–4 and an All-Star. Mike was only 2–1 and coming back from an injury.

After a scoreless first inning, the Cubs pushed across a run in the second. But Greg couldn't hold the lead, and the Phillies tied the score in the bottom of the inning.

Mike could do no better than his younger brother. The Cubs scored again in the third and took a 2–1 lead into the fourth. Then Mike Maddux settled down and put the Cubs out in order. It was up to Greg to keep the Phillies from scoring.

He couldn't. The Phillies bunched three hits around a sacrifice bunt by Mike Maddux and scored three runs. The older brother led, 4–2.

Mike began pitching the way Greg had in the first half of the season; Greg continued to struggle. When the Phillies scored twice more in the seventh, Cubs manager Don Zimmer pulled him from the game. The Phillies went on to win, 6–3. The Maddux brothers were now even at a game apiece.

Greg pitched and lost again before finally notching his sixteenth victory with a 6–5 win over the New York Mets on August 10. His slump was finally over.

Greg finished the season with eighteen wins and only eight losses. Although he was disappointed with his second-half performance, he knew he was a much better pitcher than he had been the season before. Although he had failed to win regularly after the All-Star game, he hadn't become frustrated and started throwing fastballs down the middle. He had matured and gained confidence in his own abilities. Instead of trying to change, he had continued to pitch the same way he had in the first half of the year and eventually worked his way out of the slump.

"In the first half, I got every break in the book,"

Greg said later. "In the second half, I didn't get the breaks. I just didn't win. No excuses."

It wouldn't be long before the rest of the National League would be scrambling for excuses when Greg pitched.

Chapter Seven
1989–1990

Playoffs and Problems

The Cubs were much improved in 1989. Greg pitched well all season long. While he wasn't quite as good as he had been in the first half of the 1988 season, neither was he as bad as he had been in the second half.

Now he was Mr. Consistency. Every five days, he took the mound for the Cubs and gave them a chance to win.

And the Cubs did just that. Led by outfielder Andre Dawson, second baseman Ryne Sandberg, and first baseman Mark Grace, Chicago's potent offense took advantage of the opportunities Greg provided. Fellow starting pitchers Rick Sutcliffe and Mike Bielecki followed Greg's lead and chipped in sixteen wins each. When the regular season ended, the Cubs were the surprising champions of the

National League's Eastern Division for the first time since 1984.

A week before the season ended, all eyes turned to Greg Maddux. He had just won his nineteenth regular-season game. Winning twenty games in one season for a pitcher is like hitting .300 for a batter. It proves that you're a star.

But the Cubs wanted Greg to start the first game of the playoffs instead of playing his twentieth game. It had been a long season, and they wanted to make sure he was well rested. Would Greg be willing to give up the chance at such an important regular-season milestone?

Manager Don Zimmer called Greg into his office. He planned to ask Greg to consider skipping his final start of the regular season in order to be ready to pitch against the San Francisco Giants in the playoffs.

Greg beat Zimmer to the punch. He walked into the manager's office and said, "Skipper, it would be better for the team if I rest up for the Giants. Winning twenty games isn't as important as trying to reach the World Series."

Even players on other teams were impressed by

Greg's unselfishness. St. Louis Cardinals pitcher Joe Magrane summed up the feelings of many players throughout the league when he said, "It says something about Maddux, what he did."

Greg's teammates concurred. When Andre Dawson learned what Greg had done, the veteran said simply, "Greg Maddux? I'll play behind him anytime."

The Cubs faced the powerful San Francisco Giants in the playoffs. Led by a trio of power hitters — Kevin Mitchell, Will Clark, and Matt Williams — the Giants stood between the Cubs and Chicago's first appearance in the World Series since 1945.

Greg looked forward to pitching in the postseason. He knew that he wouldn't ever be considered a really great player until he had proven himself in a World Series.

Greg started the first game of the best-of-seven series against the Giants. Little Wrigley Field was packed to capacity as he walked out to the mound. The Giants' first hitter, outfielder Brett Butler, greeted him with a single. Butler was sacrificed to second, then Greg threw a wild pitch, and Butler advanced to third.

Greg drew a deep breath. He felt strong, but he didn't have his usual control. He knew he was in for a battle.

Will Clark stepped up to the plate for San Francisco. All season long, he had provided the big hits. He did so again. Greg left a pitch over the plate, and Clark spanked it down the right field line for a double, scoring Butler and giving the Giants a one-run lead.

The hit unnerved Greg. Kevin Mitchell followed with a single, and then Matt Williams drove both runners home with another double. Suddenly, the Giants were ahead, 3–0.

Greg finally settled down and got out of the inning without giving up another run. But now the Cubs would have to come from behind to win.

With one out, Ryne Sandberg smacked a double. Then Mark Grace homered, and the score was 3–2. The Cubs were back in the game!

But Greg just wasn't pitching well. He gave up another run in the third when Clark hit a home run. Although the Cubs answered with a run of their own to make the score 4–3, Greg wasn't able to keep San Francisco from scoring.

In the fourth inning, everything came apart. Two singles and a walk loaded the bases for San Francisco with two outs. At the plate was Will Clark. The crowd at Wrigley Field stood and cheered for Greg as he stared in at the slugging first baseman. He took the sign from the catcher, wound up, and threw.

Thwack! As Clark's bat met the ball, the crowd turned silent. Right fielder Andrew Dawson didn't even move as Clark's blast soared over his head and into the right field stands for a grand slam home run. The Giants led, 8–3.

Greg retired the next hitter on a ground ball to end the inning, but the damage was done. Manager Zimmer replaced him in the fifth.

With a big lead, the Giants pitching staff held Chicago scoreless the rest of the game and won, 11–3.

After the game, Greg didn't make any excuses. "I felt good in the bullpen [warming up before the game]," he said. "I just didn't have good command of some of my pitches." Of the grand slam to Clark, he added, "I tried to get a fastball in, and got it over instead."

Demonstrating his classic "mechanics," Greg Maddux fires in a pitch.

Greg Maddux sets a new record by pitching seven putouts in one game. He also led his team, the Chicago Cubs, to a 4–0 shutout win over the Los Angeles Dodgers.

Eye on the plate, Greg Maddux rears back for a pitch.

Every pitch counted in this game against the Pittsburgh Pirates; Greg Maddux led the Cubs to victory and chalked up a milestone twentieth win of the 1992 season.

Greg Maddux (with his wife, Kathy) is all smiles after winning the 1992 Cy Young Award.

Greg Maddux with fellow Atlanta Braves pitchers Tom Glavine (left) and John Smoltz (middle).

Greg Maddux rifles one in as pitcher for the 1994 National League
All-Star team.

In the National League, pitchers often take their turns at the plate. Greg Maddux warms up before batting practice.

A look of fierce concentration crosses Greg Maddux's face as he releases a pitch.

All eyes are on Greg Maddux during every pitch of Game Five of the 1995 World Series.

Greg Maddux's Year-to-Year Major League Baseball Statistics

Year	Team	Wins	Losses	ERA	Strikeouts	Base on Balls
*1986	Chicago Cubs	2	4	5.52	20	11
*1987	Chicago Cubs	6	14	5.61	101	74
1988	Chicago Cubs	18	8	3.18	140	81
1989	Chicago Cubs	19	12	2.95	135	82
1990	Chicago Cubs	15	5	3.46	144	71
1991	Chicago Cubs	15	11	3.35	198	66
1992	Chicago Cubs	20	11	2.18	199	70
1993	Atlanta Braves	20	10	2.36	197	52
1994	Atlanta Braves	16	6	1.56	156	31
1995	Atlanta Braves	19	2	1.63	181	23

*Played part of the year in the minors

Greg Maddux's Career Highlights

1988: Member of the National League All-Star Team

1990: National League Gold Glove Award for Fielding
as a Pitcher

1991: National League Gold Glove Award for Fielding
as a Pitcher
Led the National League in total innings

1992: Cy Young Award
National League Gold Glove Award for Fielding
as a Pitcher
Led the National League in total innings
Member of the National League All-Star Team

1993: Cy Young Award
National League Gold Glove Award for Fielding
as a Pitcher
Led the National League in total innings
Led the National League in complete games

1994: Cy Young Award
National League Gold Glove Award for Fielding
as a Pitcher
Led the National League in total innings
Led the National League in complete games
Led the National League in shutouts (three)
Member of the National League All-Star Team

1995: Cy Young Award
National League Gold Glove Award for Fielding
as a Pitcher
Led the National League in total innings
Led the National League in complete games
Led the National League in shutouts (three)
Player of the Year

When a reporter asked him if the loss had demoralized the team, Greg bristled. "Demoralize us? I don't think so. We've been coming back all season. I don't see any reason we can't now."

The next day, the Cubs proved Greg right. They battered San Francisco starting pitcher Rick Reuschel for six first-inning runs and went on to win, 9–5.

The Giants won Game Three in San Francisco, 5–4, to go up two games to one. Greg took the mound in Game Four knowing that if he didn't win, the Cubs would be down three games to one, a nearly insurmountable deficit.

But for the second game in a row, Greg struggled. This time it was Matt Williams who gave him trouble, knocking in two runs in the third with a single, then knocking Greg from the game with a home run in the fifth to break a 4–4 tie and put the Giants ahead for good, 6–4.

The next day, it was all over. The Giants won, 3–2, and earned the right to face the Oakland Athletics in the World Series. The Cubs' season had ended.

Greg was disappointed. He hadn't just pitched poorly. He had pitched terribly. In just over seven innings, he had given up 13 hits and 11 earned runs.

That made him even more motivated the following season. He wanted to pitch well all year long.

By the time spring training rolled around in 1990, Greg was feeling optimistic. He had finished third in voting for the National League's Cy Young Award, and the Cubs had rewarded him for his 19–12 record with a new contract worth $2.4 million. Virtually every player from the 1989 division champs team was returning. Greg believed they had a good chance to repeat their success. This year, he hoped, the Cubs would reach the World Series.

Once again, Greg got off to a fast start, winning four of his first five starts. His performance was particularly important as the Cubs' other pitchers struggled. In early May, Greg was the main reason the Cubs' record hovered around .500. Without him, they would have been in last place.

Then, without warning, it was like the 1988 season all over again. The *second* half of the 1988 season.

Every five or six days, Greg took the mound and no matter how he pitched, he couldn't win. If the Cubs scored five runs, Greg gave up six. If the Cubs scored two runs, Greg gave up three. When he did pitch well, as he did in a game against the Montreal

Expos in mid-June, he suffered a loss of concentration that cost him a win.

In this game against the Expos, Greg entered the eighth inning with a 2–0 lead. He retired the first two hitters, then went up on outfielder Larry Walker two strikes and no balls.

Pitching coach Dick Pole signaled from the bench that he wanted Greg to throw a pitch outside. But Greg thought otherwise. He wanted to throw a pitch inside. Somehow, Greg and catcher Joe Girardi got their signals crossed. Girardi was still looking for a ball outside when Greg's pitch sailed in.

Walker swung for strike three, but Girardi missed the ball. When the catcher doesn't catch strike three, the hitter is allowed to run, and the catcher must try to throw him out.

As the ball rolled toward the backstop, Walker took off. Girardi had trouble coming up with the ball. Walker rounded first and went all the way to second. Instead of being out of the inning, Montreal now had a man in scoring position.

Greg's concentration was shot. He walked the next man and then gave up two singles. The Expos scored three runs and won, 3–2.

After the loss, Cubs manager Don Zimmer was livid. "You wonder why he's 4–8?" he yelled to reporters after the game. "He didn't pay attention. For two years, his pitching coach has been helping him, and he's won thirty-seven games. Now he wants to throw it his way. If that's what he wants to do, he's going to be 4–14."

For a while, it looked as if Zimmer was right. At the All-Star break several weeks later, Greg still hadn't won another game. Needless to say, he didn't make the All-Star team.

Greg's problem was a combination of bad luck and the facts that the other Cubs pitchers were struggling and that Greg was trying to pitch perfectly. Every time he made a mistake, it seemed to cost him a win.

Greg made thirteen straight starts without winning a single game. Over the stretch he was 0–8 with an ERA of more than 6.00. In the press, sportswriters began to question the wisdom of giving Greg a big contract. In their opinion, Greg no longer seemed to have what it takes to be the number one pitcher on a team. The number one pitcher on a team is supposed to be a "stopper," the player who stops losing streaks. Perhaps, the sportswriters wondered, Greg Maddux couldn't take the pressure. After all, hadn't he pitched poorly in the playoffs the year before?

Finally, on July 18, Greg pitched seven strong innings against the San Diego Padres. The Cubs won, 4–2, giving Greg the fiftieth win of his career and improving his season record to 5–9.

That's all it took. The win settled Greg down, and he regained his confidence. He was still pitching the way he had in 1988 — only now he was pitching the way he had during the *first* half of 1988.

For the next month, it was almost impossible to score a run off Greg. He notched five straight wins. Though he cooled after that, he was 11–7 in the second half and finished the season with a record of 15–15. Not Cy Young material, but better than he could have hoped for at midseason.

But Greg's turnaround was too little, too late for the Cubs. They finished tied for fourth place with a record of 77–85, eighteen games behind the division champion Pittsburgh Pirates. Cubs fans spent the winter as they had every season since 1908: They were "waiting till next year."

Chapter Eight
1991-1992

Chasing the Dream

At the beginning of the 1991 spring training season, Greg told a sportswriter about his dream.

"I think about it in the car, in bed, all the time," he said. "We're in Wrigley Field, and I'm on the field as the game ends. The place is going crazy, like you've never seen it before."

"Who are you playing?" asked the writer.

Greg grinned at him. "It's an American League team," he said.

The writer just nodded. He understood. Greg's dream was about winning the World Series.

Greg knew that no matter what he was able to accomplish personally, until he led his team to the World Series, people would always question his ability. More than anything else, that's precisely what he wanted to do.

But all the 1991 season did for Cubs fans was make them wait another season. Greg's dream remained just that, a dream.

He pitched well, but he didn't receive much help from his teammates. Apart from Greg, none of the Cubs pitchers played very well.

In 1991, Greg was able to avoid the bad half-seasons that had marred both the 1988 and 1990 seasons. He won fifteen games, lost only eleven, and had an ERA of just over three runs a game. But the Cubs still finished in fourth place, twenty games behind Pittsburgh.

At age twenty-five, Greg found his career at a crossroad. His contract was up, and he began to consider his options. He wanted to sign a long-term deal that would allow him to plan for his future.

Greg's agent told the Cubs that Greg was expecting a contract for four or five years worth about $5 million per year. After all, Greg reasoned, his sixty-seven wins over the past four seasons were the best in the National League.

The two sides started to negotiate. In the meantime, Greg and his wife, Kathy, started looking for a home in the Chicago area. If Greg signed a long-term deal, the couple planned to move from Las Vegas.

After a few weeks, the two sides came to an agreement. Then the Cubs suddenly changed their mind and balked at inking Greg to a long-term contract.

The Cubs knew that according to baseball's rules, Greg wouldn't be able to become a free agent, a player not under contract by any team, until after the 1992 season. They didn't have to sign him to a big, long-term contract right away. Besides, Greg still hadn't put together two consecutive good years without forgetting how to pitch for half a season. If Greg stumbled in 1992, the Cubs figured they might be able to sign him to a long-term deal for a lot less money.

Greg was upset. He didn't think it was fair for the Cubs to change their minds. They finally offered Greg a one-year contract and promised to try to negotiate a longer deal with his agent during the season. Greg didn't have much choice. He accepted the deal.

Although the contract was for only one season, it was still quite a contract! In the spring of 1992, the Cubs signed Greg to a one-year deal worth $4.2 million, the biggest contract in the history of the Cubs and one of the best in baseball.

Greg finally came to the conclusion that the deal actually worked to his advantage. If he and the Cubs could agree to a long-term deal, that would be great. If Greg had a winning year, the Cubs would have to pay him even more. And if they couldn't agree on a deal, he would then be free to play for any team he wanted.

The only concern Greg had about remaining in Chicago was his dream. He knew he didn't want to stay if the Cubs weren't good enough to win the pennant. But by signing for just one year, Greg gave the Cubs a season to improve — and gave himself a way out if they didn't.

In spring training, Greg pitched better than he ever had before. When the season started, he kept pitching that way.

On the mound, he was all business. He didn't yell at himself anymore or show up the opposition. Greg was in control of more than his pitches. He was in control of himself, too. As a result, he remained focused on precisely what he wanted to do with each pitch and didn't get distracted.

Unfortunately, Greg was just about the only Cubs pitcher who was playing well. Although he won all four of his starts in April, the other Cubs pitchers won a total of only three games, and the Cubs finished the month with a record of 7–13. The season had hardly started, and they were already eight games out of first place.

Greg pitched well all season long, but he didn't receive much help from his teammates. He had to pitch almost perfectly in order to win.

At midseason, although his record was only 10–8, everyone agreed that Greg was the best pitcher in the league. His earned run average was just over 2.00. Hitters were barely hitting for a .200 batting average against him. For the second time in his career, Greg made the All-Star team.

This time he got to play, pitching one and a third innings, and giving up a single run. Although Greg was a little disappointed in his performance, he was happy to have made the team.

During the three-day All-Star break, Greg did some thinking. The Cubs were mired in fourth place, far behind the division-leading Pittsburgh Pirates. It didn't look as if the team would be able to contend for a pennant for several seasons, no matter how well Greg pitched.

He was also disappointed in his contract negotiations with the team. Basically, the club was offering him the same deal they had backed out of at the beginning of the season. In the end, Greg had to consider his own future ahead of the Cubs.

"I'm going to go ahead and become a free agent at the end of the year," he told a reporter. "I wouldn't say I'm bitter. I'm just disappointed."

Knowing that it was unlikely he would ever pitch for the Cubs again, Greg pitched even better in the second half of the season. Although the Cubs didn't give him much run support, Greg won anyway. If the Cubs scored two runs, Greg gave up one. He only seemed to lose when the pitcher on the other team threw a shutout. That happened seven times in 1992.

Greg pitched particularly well in September, winning four of five starts to improve his record to 19–11. With only one start left, Greg had a second chance to win twenty games while playing for the Cubs.

On October 1, the division champion Pittsburgh Pirates came to Chicago. Greg took the mound.

He knew it wouldn't be easy to win his twentieth game. The Pirates were one of the best teams in baseball, led by Barry Bonds, one of the best players in the game.

Although Greg struggled early, he kept the Pirates from scoring. Meanwhile, the Cubs scratched out six runs to give Greg a 6–0 lead. In the eighth inning, the Pirates had runners on first and third with two outs. Catcher Tom Prince was at bat.

Greg wound up and threw. The pitch fooled Prince, but he still managed to get his bat on the ball and hit a soft line drive back toward Greg.

One of the benefits of Greg's pitching motion is that after he throws the ball, he is in near perfect position to field. In fact, Greg is such a good fielder that he has won the Gold Glove award as the best fielding pitcher in the National League every year since 1990.

As Prince's hit came toward him, Greg reached out instinctively for the ball. But it was just out of reach and ticked off the end of his glove. The ball rolled slowly into no-man's-land between the pitcher's mound and second base. Prince raced toward first with an apparent hit as the Pirates runner on third dashed home. It looked as if the run would score and the Pirates might go on to have a big inning.

But Greg hadn't won the Gold Glove award for nothing. He wheeled around and sprinted after the ball. Although the ball was rolling away from him, Greg was still able to reach beyond it and gather the slow roller into his mitt.

The runner on first was already at second base, and the runner on third was about to cross home. Greg's only play was to nab Prince at first base.

He grabbed the ball and skidded to a stop. In one motion he spun completely around and fired the ball toward first baseman Mark Grace. The throw was perfect. Prince and the ball appeared to arrive at the base at the same time.

The umpire hesitated for a split second, then threw his arm into the air. "Out!" Thanks to Greg's determination to go the extra mile, the inning was over. The run didn't count.

In the ninth inning, Greg set the Pirates down in order, striking out pinch hitter Gary Varsho for the game's final out. In his last appearance in a Cubs uniform, Greg had won his twentieth game of the season.

Winning twenty games is quite an accomplishment for any pitcher, but winning twenty games for a team like the Cubs is even more difficult. Not only did the team have a poor record, but tiny Wrigley Field is one of the toughest ballparks in the major leagues for a pitcher to succeed in. Pop-fly outs in other ballparks can be over-the-fence home runs in Wrigley Field.

But the way Greg pitched in 1992 made Wrigley Field seem twice as large as it was. He was the first Cubs pitcher in fifteen seasons to win twenty games. His thirty-five starts and 268 innings pitched led the National League, and his ERA for the year was a minuscule 2.18.

At the end of the season, the Cubs finally seemed to realize how important Greg was to the team. Although they had finished in fourth place with a record below .500, without Greg they would have finished last. The Cubs decided to make one more attempt to sign Greg to a contract. Despite his earlier statements, Greg agreed to listen to the Cubs one last time.

While the two sides talked, Greg's value kept increasing. Despite pitching for the fourth-place

Cubs, Greg was named the National League's Cy Young award winner, collecting twenty of twenty-four first-place votes and beating out the Atlanta Braves' star pitcher, Tom Glavine.

"To finally win this means a lot to me personally," Greg told reporters after learning he had won. "It means all the hard work has finally paid off." Then, remembering his dream, he added, "Now, the only thing left is to pitch in a World Series."

The Cubs made a final offer to Greg of $27.5 million over five years with an incentive package worth another $1 million. Greg and his agent considered the offer but finally decided to turn it down. Money wasn't everything. Greg wanted to pitch in the World Series. He knew that teams better than the Cubs would like to have him pitch for them.

The New York Yankees, of the American League, had a reputation as one of the biggest spenders in all of baseball. Yankee owner George Steinbrenner had spent millions on players, trying to bring a world championship to New York. The Yankees wanted Greg badly.

Greg, his wife, Kathy, and his agent, Scott Boras, traveled to New York to meet with the Yankees.

They were stunned when the Yankees offered Greg a six-year deal worth $37.5 million, $10 million more than the Cubs had offered!

No player in baseball had ever been offered a larger contract. Greg and Kathy tentatively agreed, then started to look around the New York area for a place to live.

But deep down, Greg wasn't sure. He had a laid-back personality, and he worried about playing in New York City, where his every move was sure to be scrutinized in the press. He also worried about pitching in the American League. He felt as if he had figured out how to pitch to all the hitters in the National League, and he didn't want to have to start over.

Then he looked at the Yankees team itself. While they were a good team, they weren't great. There was no guarantee that they would reach the World Series. The Yankees were particularly thin in the starting pitching department. Greg worried that he might end up in a situation similar to that in Chicago, where he was the best pitcher on a mediocre staff. He wasn't sure if he wanted to go through that again.

Then, at the last minute, Greg and his agent received a call from the Atlanta Braves. The Braves wanted to make him an offer.

Interest from the Braves surprised Greg. They were already one of the best teams in baseball. They had reached the World Series in both 1991 and 1992, only to lose each time. Their starting rotation was solid. Tom Glavine had won the Cy Young award in 1991, John Smoltz had led the National League in strikeouts in 1992, and Steve Avery had pitched spectacularly in the postseason in both 1991 and 1992. Greg didn't think the Braves really needed him.

But after reaching the World Series two years in a row and losing both times, Braves owner Ted Turner was getting impatient. More than anything else, he wanted to win the World Series. He knew that adding the best pitcher in baseball might be just enough to put the Braves over the top.

The Braves offered Greg only $28 million, far less than what the Yankees had offered. But Greg was intrigued. In Atlanta, he would be just another player, not the big star. He had always liked visiting the city. Besides, Atlanta was in the National

League, and he wouldn't have to learn how to pitch to a whole new set of hitters.

Greg and Kathy discussed the two offers privately. They decided to sign with the Atlanta Braves.

The Yankees were stunned. They couldn't believe a player would turn down an extra $10 million!

But Greg was that kind of player. He was already wealthier than he ever imagined he would be. And he had won nearly every individual honor baseball offered. There was only one thing missing: When Greg looked at his hand, all he saw was an empty space on his finger. He knew he wouldn't be satisfied until that space was filled by a championship ring.

The place to get that, he now believed, was in the city of Atlanta, pitching for the Braves.

Chapter Nine
1993

At Home in Atlanta

When Greg arrived at the Braves' spring training camp in late February of 1993, he immediately felt comfortable. The other Braves pitchers were happy to have him on the team and weren't at all jealous of Greg's big contract. They knew that having Greg gave the ball club an even better chance of reaching the World Series again.

Greg discovered that he had a lot in common with his new teammates, particularly with the Braves' other starting pitchers. Glavine, Smoltz, and Avery all loved to pitch. They took their job seriously and spent hours discussing pitching and picking one another's brains for tips on what to throw different hitters.

But they also knew how to have fun. In the clubhouse before and after games and in the dugout and bullpen, the pitchers needled each other and played practical jokes.

They were just as close off the field. All three loved to golf, and they were nearly as competitive on the golf course as they were on the baseball diamond.

Greg loved the atmosphere around the Braves. From the very beginning, the other starters made Greg feel at home and included him in all their activities. He enjoyed sharing his thoughts on pitching with the other pitchers, and they soon discovered that Greg took his golf game almost as seriously as he did his pitching. After only a few weeks, Greg felt as if he had been playing for the Braves his entire career. He almost forgot all about the Cubs.

But when the season started, he was reminded of his years in Chicago. Based on his stellar performance in spring training, Braves manager Bobby Cox selected Greg to pitch on opening day, the first game of the season. And guess who the Braves played? The Cubs, in Chicago! Greg's first start for his new team would be against his old team.

When Greg walked out onto Wrigley Field to warm up in the bull pen, the fans that had spent the last seven seasons cheering him greeted him with a loud chorus of boos. Cubs fans had felt cheated when Greg signed with Atlanta, and they let him know it. When the public-address announcer introduced him before the game, they booed again.

As the visiting team, the Braves came to bat first and scored a quick run to take a 1–0 lead. Then Greg took the mound.

As soon as he emerged from the dugout, the booing began again. One fan in the stands waved a huge banner back and forth that read GREG WHO?

Earlier in his career, Greg may have let such a reception bother him. He might have gotten angry, tried to throw the ball too hard, and forgotten to use his change-up. But not anymore. Greg was in control. He concentrated so hard on pitching that he hardly heard the crowd.

Cubs fans saw the same pitcher they had grown accustomed to. Inning after inning, Greg kept the Cubs scoreless. He was a master of efficiency on the mound and kept his old teammates off balance the whole game. Hitter after hitter slapped the ball into the ground for easy outs. Greg only gave up a handful of meaningless hits.

Still nursing the one-run lead in the ninth inning, Greg began to tire. With one out, he was lifted from the game. As he left the field, Cubs fans booed long and hard.

Had Greg been pitching for Chicago in a similar situation, he probably would have been left in the game. The Cubs didn't have a very good bull pen. But the Braves' pen was deep and experienced. A relief pitcher retired the final two hitters to secure the shutout and preserve Greg's win.

After the game, reporters from both Atlanta and Chicago crowded around Greg's locker and peppered him with questions.

"How'd it feel to pitch against your old teammates, Greg?" shouted one.

"Did you hear the boos? Did they bother you?" asked another.

Greg sat in front of his locker with a tired smile on his face. Yes, he admitted, he had heard the boos at first, and no, they hadn't bothered him, and yes, it was strange pitching against his old teammates. "I had knots in my stomach the whole game," he finally admitted.

From a nearby locker, Greg's catcher, Damon Berryhill, who had also been Greg's catcher with the Cubs, called over "They can get on him every time if he'll go out and throw like that."

Greg's Atlanta teammates were thrilled with his performance against the Cubs. They were more certain than ever that Greg would lead them to a world championship.

The Braves got off to a quick start, but after Greg's opening day victory, he had a hard time earning a win. Greg pitched well his next five starts, but he lost or failed to get a decision in all but one game.

In mid-May, the Braves faced the Philadelphia Phillies. At the time, the Phillies had the best record in baseball. Although the Braves had won six of their last seven games, they were in second place in the National League's Western Division, trailing the surprisingly strong San Francisco Giants. Although it was early in the year, the contest against Philadelphia was already a big game. The Braves couldn't afford to fall too far behind the Giants.

Once again, Greg pitched well, but in the eighth inning he trailed, 3–2.

The bases were loaded, with two outs. The Phillies' Wes Chamberlain stood at the plate, waving his bat at Greg.

If Greg had learned one thing playing for the Braves, it was that they played as a team. Unlike the Cubs, the Braves had a good player at every position. Greg knew he could depend on his defense, even with two outs and the bases loaded in a close game. He didn't have to strike Chamberlain out.

He wound up and threw. Chamberlain was guessing on the pitch, and he guessed right. *Crack!* He smoked a sharp ground ball down the third base line. The crowd gasped. It sounded like a sure base hit.

But Atlanta third baseman Terry Pendleton had another idea. He was playing close to the line. He dove to his right after the ball, sprawling on the ground in a cloud of dust. He caught it! But he still had to throw the batter out.

Pendleton scrambled to his feet and threw toward Braves first baseman Sid Bream. The other Phillies runners scrambled around the bases as Chamberlain dashed down the first base line and dove headfirst for the bag. If he made it safely, the

Phillies would score, take a two-run lead, and still have the bases loaded.

Bream stretched out as far as he could and snagged Pendleton's throw as Chamberlain arrived at the base in a cloud of dust. "Out!" signaled the umpire. Greg looked over at Pendleton and gave a great big sigh of relief. The inning was over.

But the Braves still had to score two runs in order for Greg to get the win. They didn't want to let him down.

They didn't. The Braves rallied for three runs, and Atlanta won, 5–3, giving Greg a much-needed victory and allowing Atlanta to keep pace with the Giants.

When Greg talked with reporters after the game, he sounded a familiar theme. "I've accomplished everything I want to personally," he said. "The only thing I haven't done is pitch in the World Series and get that ring. That's why I'm here."

Greg remained focused on his goal through the remainder of the season.

But no matter how well the Braves played, they couldn't seem to catch the Giants. Greg did all he could. In the second half of the season, he pitched even better than he had in the first half. The Braves started scoring runs when he pitched. Yet despite his winning four of five starts in August and an ERA of only 1.53, at the beginning of September the Braves still trailed San Francisco by a few games.

It was a pennant race, and both teams knew it. No matter where the Braves were playing, they kept one eye on the scoreboard to check and see how the Giants were doing. San Francisco's players did the same thing. Members of both teams knew that every game was crucial. In a tight pennant race, one game could make the difference between reaching the World Series and spending late October at home on the couch watching it on TV.

Greg carried the team in September, winning almost every time he took the mound. With only two days left in the season, the Giants and the Braves were tied for first place. Each had already won an amazing 102 games.

Greg pitched against the Colorado Rockies with a chance to win his twentieth regular-season game. But he wasn't concerned about that. He only knew that he had to win to give his team a crack at the division title.

The Rockies didn't have a chance. Atlanta's big bats exploded for ten runs, and Greg pitched a typical Greg Maddux game, giving up only four hits and a single run. Meanwhile, the Giants beat the Dodgers, 5–3. With only one game left in the season, the Giants and the Braves were still tied for first place.

"It's exciting," said Greg after the game. "This is what it's all about." Then, perhaps thinking of all those seasons he had spent with the Cubs when they were out of the pennant race by midsummer, he added, "It's nice to pitch late in the season, when it counts."

Greg hoped his season was far from over. If the Braves and the Giants ended it the next day still tied for first place, there would be a one-game playoff in San Francisco. Even though Greg would have only one day of rest, he knew he might have to pitch.

"I expect to go to San Francisco," he told reporters. "We have to expect to win Sunday and be ready to go there and play."

But before the Braves could contemplate a trip to San Francisco, they had to play the Rockies again in the final game of the season. At the same time, the Giants would be playing the Los Angeles Dodgers. If either team won and the other lost, the winning team would capture the division title. There would be no need for a playoff.

There was one big difference between the Braves and the Giants, and that difference proved to be critical in the deciding matchups. Pitching. The Braves had it and the Giants didn't, at least not as much as Atlanta. While the Braves were able to start Tom Glavine, a Cy Young Award winner, against the Rockies, the Giants had to pitch a rookie, Salomon Torres, against the Dodgers.

After all the speculation about a tiebreaker game, the last day of the season was anticlimactic. The experienced Glavine stopped the Rockies, and the Braves won, 5–3. The inexperienced Torres was shelled, and the Giants lost 12–1 to the Dodgers. The Braves were division champions.

After two days off, the Braves traveled to Philadelphia to meet the Eastern Division champion Phillies. Last place finishers the year before, the Phillies had come from nowhere in 1993 to race to the division title. The two teams would play a best-of-seven-game series to determine who would have the right to play the American League champions in the World Series.

The Braves were big favorites. After all, they had four of the best pitchers in all of baseball and a batting lineup that included swift slugger Ron Gant, heavy hitters David Justice and Fred McGriff, and Terry Pendleton, who had won the MVP award in 1991. On paper, the Braves looked invincible.

But the Phillies knew that baseball games aren't won or lost on paper. If that were the case, they'd have finished last again, which was what everyone had predicted at the beginning of the season. The Phillies had played hard all year long. Paced by lead-off hitter and center fielder Lenny Dykstra and their consistent first baseman, John Kruk, the Phils had scrapped and fought for every run all season. While their pitching staff didn't include any Greg Madduxes or Tom Glavines, nearly everyone had contributed with the best season of his career.

The series opened in Philadelphia on Wednesday, October 6. Any ideas the Braves had about being invincible didn't last the day.

Steve Avery started for the Braves. He pitched well, but so did Phillies starter Curt Schilling. Both were replaced when the Braves tied the score 3–3 in the ninth inning.

With one out in the tenth, John Kruk doubled off Braves reliever Greg McMichael. When Kim Batiste followed with a single, Kruk scored and gave the Phillies a 4–3 win.

The Braves didn't panic. They knew Greg Maddux was pitching game two.

Despite his stellar season, Greg was anxious before the game. It had been four long years since he had pitched in the division playoffs for the Cubs, and he wanted to do well.

His teammates gave him some immediate help. At the top of the first inning, Fred McGriff cracked a monstrous two-run home run into the upper deck of Philadelphia's Veterans Stadium to put the Braves ahead 2–0.

But the Phillies didn't give up. Two of their first three hitters reached base on a base hit and a walk.

Greg knew that this was an important time in the game. McGriff's blast had quieted the Philadelphia crowd, but now they were on their feet and roaring again. Greg wanted to keep them quiet.

He worked carefully on cleanup hitter Dave

Hollins. He didn't want to give him a chance to pull the ball for a home run, so he tried to pitch outside. His control would have to be perfect.

It was. Hollins tried to pull an outside pitch and lofted an easy fly ball to center field for out number two. Then Greg completely fooled the next hitter, Darren Daulton, striking him out to end the inning.

That was just about the ball game. The Braves exploded for six runs in the third inning, and Greg remained in command from there on, pitching seven innings and giving up only five hits. The Braves eventually won, 14–3. The series was tied, and Greg had the first postseason win of his career.

Greg was delighted after the game. He liked pitching when his team scored a lot of runs.

"It's really great when they do that," he told reporters. "Then you just try to throw strikes. You enjoy it as a pitcher."

Tom Glavine had all the fun when the Braves returned to Atlanta for game three. The Braves scored nine runs for him in their 9–4 win to go up in the series two games to one. With John Smoltz scheduled to pitch game four, the Braves felt they had the series under control.

But their bats went silent in game four and the Braves lost, 2–1. Then, in game five, the Braves tied the game at 3–3 with three ninth-inning runs, only to lose it in the tenth when Lenny Dykstra hit a home run. Suddenly the Phillies led the series three games to two. If the Braves lost once more, their dream of reaching the World Series would be over.

The two teams returned to Philadelphia. The Braves handed the ball to Greg Maddux in game six.

With one out in the first inning, Philadelphia second baseman Mickey Morandini hit a vicious line drive right back at Greg. He tried to reach the ball with his glove, but it ricocheted off his right calf.

Greg scrambled after the ball and threw Morandini out, but for the remainder of the game the leg bothered him. Uncharacteristically, Greg struggled with his control.

That was the only break the opportunistic Phillies needed. They scored twice in the third inning, twice in the fifth, and twice more in the sixth before Greg was removed from the game. Those six runs were the most he had given up all season long.

This time, the Atlanta offense couldn't keep up.

Three Philadelphia pitchers combined to hold the Braves to only five hits and three runs. The Philadelphia Phillies became the National League champions and won the right to play in the World Series. All the Braves won was the right to think about next year.

After the game, Greg Maddux made no excuses. Although he admitted that the leg hurt, he insisted it had nothing to do with the way he pitched.

"I still think we're the better team," he said, "But they beat us, and you have to give them credit. Our goal was to win the World Series, not just get there. Unfortunately, we didn't get there."

Getting there and winning was still the only goal Greg Maddux really cared about. But he didn't yet realize how difficult that was going to be.

Chapter Ten
1994

The Wrong Kind of Strike

It wasn't until Greg returned home to Las Vegas in the off-season that he began to realize exactly how well he had pitched in 1993. Not only had he won twenty games for the second year in a row, but he again led the National League in games completed and innings pitched. He threw 197 strikeouts, and his 2.36 ERA led the league. This, combined with his spectacular pitching the year before, had everyone starting to realize that perhaps Greg was not just a great pitcher, but one of the best pitchers of all time.

In early November, Greg was rewarded with his second consecutive Cy Young Award, becoming, after Sandy Koufax, Jim Palmer, and Roger Clemens, only the fourth pitcher ever to win the award in two consecutive seasons. When he was told he had won, Greg was characteristically reserved.

"I never really thought of myself as that kind of pitcher," he said. "I feel I'm capable of winning, but those guys all threw in the upper nineties [when they won the award]. I'm not capable of doing that.

"It's the ultimate goal," he added, "aside from winning the World Series."

In early December, Greg and Kathy celebrated the birth of their first child, a girl they named Amanda. But before too long, it was back to spring training to prepare for the 1994 season.

Spring training didn't go as planned for the Braves. Outfielder Ron Gant and rookie phenom Chipper Jones were lost for the season with injuries, while relief pitcher Gregg Olson and starter Steve Avery were saddled with arm problems. Even Greg got into the act, scaring the Braves in his last spring start by taking another line drive off his leg. The Braves, odds-on favorites to win the National League pennant, suddenly looked beatable.

But baseball had changed the divisional setup and the postseason schedule. The National League had added teams in Colorado and Florida, so they created a Central Division and realigned the East and West. The Braves moved from the West to the East.

It had also been decided that the winners of all three divisions would make the playoffs, as well as one team with the best record that didn't win a division title. This wild-card spot gave the Braves an extra chance to reach the World Series.

By opening day, Greg had recovered from the leg injury and pitched his usual game. He gave up only six hits, and the Braves beat the San Diego Padres, 4–1.

The win sparked the Braves to their best start in Atlanta history. The club won thirteen of its first fourteen games to surge into first place. It looked as if there was no way to keep the Braves from winning the division, the pennant, and the World Series.

But the Braves had trouble after their quick start and stumbled. The Montreal Expos started playing well, and as spring turned into summer, the Expos were breathing down the Braves' necks.

The way Greg was pitching, however, the Braves needed to score only a run or two each game in order to win. He was better than ever.

Just before the All-Star break, Greg's record was 11–2 and his ERA was well under 2.00. Everyone, it seemed, was jumping on the Greg Maddux bandwagon. Writers were starting to compare him to some of baseball's all-time greats, Hall of Famers like Grover Cleveland Alexander and Christy Mathewson, stellar pitchers from baseball's early days.

Even his own teammates were in awe of how well Greg was pitching. When asked to describe how he pitched, Braves catcher Javy Lopez replied simply, "Got everything. I mean, I haven't seen him throw a straight fastball yet."

Greg made the All-Star team and was selected to start the game, an honor usually reserved for the best pitcher among all the All-Stars. He pitched well, giving up only a single run in three innings.

But not all was right with the Braves. On the last day before the All-Star break, they fell to second place behind the Expos. And a darker cloud than that hung on the horizon. The entire baseball season ground to a halt on August 12.

All season long, players from both leagues had been working without an agreement with the owners of major league baseball. Although both the players and owners were making a lot of money, each side thought it should receive an even larger piece of baseball's financial pie. The players were threatening to do the unthinkable: unless an agreement was reached, they would lay down their bats and gloves and go on strike.

On August 12, 1994, they carried out their threat. By striking so late in the season, the players hoped the owners would come to a quick settlement. After all, the World Series was right around the corner. But as the days turned to weeks, then over a month, neither side seemed willing to move.

The Braves did manage to end their brief season on a high note. Greg took the mound on August 12 in Denver, Colorado, against the Colorado Rockies, one of the best hitting teams in baseball. If this was going to be the last game of the season, Greg wanted to make it his best.

It was. He gave up only three hits, and the Braves pummeled the Rockies, 13–0. At one stretch, Greg went almost three full innings without the umpire calling a pitch a ball. He didn't walk anyone and won his sixteenth game while dropping his ERA to 1.56. Both figures led the league.

After the game, the players went on strike. Although no team could beat Greg Maddux, not even he could end the baseball strike. Over the outraged cries of the fans nationwide, the two sides dug in. Each underestimated the resolve of the other. In the end, the rest of the season was canceled. For the first time in more than ninety years, no World Series was played.

Greg's dream would have to wait at least one more year.

Chapter Eleven
1995

Almost Perfect

All Greg could do was wait for the strike to end. He returned home to Las Vegas and tried to stay in shape.

The only bright spot of the entire winter came in early November. For an unprecedented third season in a row, Greg was awarded the National League's Cy Young Award. All twenty-eight sportswriters who voted for the award gave Greg a first-place vote.

But no award could make up for not being able to play baseball and not having the chance to live out his dream.

It wasn't until the following April that the strike finally ended. A federal judge decided that the baseball owners had broken the rules during the strike. The players approved returning to a previous agreement, and everyone rushed to an abbreviated spring training. Whether the fans would be waiting for them — or were still too angry to support baseball this season — remained to be seen.

Greg had stayed in shape and didn't need much time to get ready for the season. But in spring training, he got sick. Greg Maddux, the best pitcher in baseball, got the chicken pox! Fortunately, he made a quick recovery. When the season opened on April 26, Greg was on the mound for the Braves.

In his first appearance since the previous August, he turned in a midseason performance. The Braves erupted for a quick 7–0 lead, and Greg gave up only a single run in five innings of work in the eventual 12–6 Atlanta victory. The season was only one day old, and Greg and the Braves were both 1–0.

Then, impossibly, Greg started getting even better. He just kept winning and winning and winning. On May 29, he nearly reached perfection. It was just the kind of superstar performance the sport needed to woo the fans back once and for all.

Pitching against the Houston Astros in the Astrodome, Greg was in almost total command. His fastball was moving, and he was able to throw it exactly where he wanted to. His change-up had rarely been better. Even his curveball was working well.

Inning after inning, Greg set the Astros down in order. Batter after batter beat the ball into the ground, where the Braves infielders scooped it up then threw the Astros hitters out at first. Entering the eighth inning, the Braves led, 2–0.

No one sat next to Greg on the Braves bench between innings or said a word to him. That would have been considered bad luck, because Greg was pitching a no-hitter!

When Greg took the mound to start the eighth inning, the Astros' first hitter, Jeff Bagwell, dug in. Greg knew he had to be careful. Bagwell was one of the best hitters in baseball.

He thought Bagwell would expect him to try to throw the ball outside, as he had last time Bagwell had batted. Instead, Greg decided to throw Bagwell an inside fastball.

The crowd inside the Astrodome stood and cheered. Watching someone try for a no-hitter, even if it is an opposing player, is always exciting.

Greg threw. Bagwell started to swing.

As soon as the ball left Greg's hand, he wanted to

take it back. For the first time all game, he hadn't put the pitch exactly where he wanted to. The ball wasn't far enough inside.

Crack! Bagwell hit the ball with the fat part of his bat and drove it over the left field wall for a home run. The no-hitter and the shutout were gone. Now the Braves led by only a single run.

Some pitchers would have been bothered after giving up a home run in such a situation. But it didn't distract Greg. Although the home run didn't make him happy, neither did he allow it to make him lose his focus. After all, his goal was to win this game, because that would help the Braves win the pennant and reach the World Series. Nothing else mattered.

No other Astro reached base. The Braves went on to win, 3–1. Greg had thrown only ninety-seven pitches in the entire game. Including Bagwell's home run, only four balls had been hit out of the infield all game.

"Hey," said Greg after the game, "I'm happy to throw a one-hitter. This game has been so good to me, there's no way I could ever ask for more."

Except, of course, a World Series ring.

The Braves briefly dropped into second place, then started playing well again in June, regaining possession of first place in the National League East. For the remainder of the season, as the Braves increased their lead over the other teams in their division, Brave fans knew they could count on one thing. Every fifth day, when Greg Maddux pitched, Atlanta was virtually unbeatable.

For the second year in a row, Greg was selected to the National League All-Star team. Because of his stellar record, everyone expected Greg to be picked to start the game.

But Dodgers pitcher Hideo Nomo, playing his first year in the United States after starring in Japan, had become a fan favorite. Greg knew that the All-Star game would be the first chance many fans around the country would have to see Nomo pitch.

A few days before the game, Greg claimed to have a slight leg injury. Though he would suit up for the game, he said it would be better to rest his leg rather than pitch. Few people in baseball believed that Greg's leg was really hurt. They understood what he was doing. He was giving everyone a chance to see Nomo. Besides, Greg had already started an All-Star game. He wanted Nomo to have the same opportunity.

In late August, as the Braves moved closer to clinching the division championship, Greg threw what he considers to be one of the best games of his major league career.

The Braves were in St. Louis, playing the Cardinals, and had lost their last three games. Greg had missed his last start with the flu. Now the team looked to him to end its losing streak.

He did just that. He stopped the Cardinals cold. After retiring the first twelve hitters he faced, he gave up a single to outfielder Brian Jordan. Then Greg retired the next three hitters to end the threat.

In the sixth inning, he gave up another hit when Danny Shaeffer doubled off the wall. But that was it. No one else reached base.

Greg threw only eighty-eight pitches, including a remarkable sixty-six for strikes. He didn't walk a hitter and he struck out nine, a season high. His season record improved to 13–2 as the Braves won, 1–0.

"That is as good as I can pitch," he admitted after the game. "It's nice to be able to say that."

Greg was pitching so well he was beginning to set some kind of record every time he took the mound. In September, he beat Cincinnati, 6–1, and set a major league mark by winning his seventeenth consecutive decision on the road.

His coach, teammates, and even the opposition couldn't say enough about how well Greg was pitching. "There is no new adjective to describe Mr. Maddux," quipped Braves manager Bobby Cox. Added New York Mets manager Dallas Green a few weeks later, "Every hitter in the game has a pitch he can't handle. Maddux knows where that pitch is on every hitter and puts the ball right there."

Greg didn't let his success in the regular season go to his head. Just before the end of the year, he commented to a reporter, "I try to keep things in perspective. Our season's not over, we haven't accomplished our goal yet, and I don't want this to get in the way of anything."

The Braves ended the regular season with a record of 90–54, first in the National League East and twenty-one games ahead of the second-place Phillies. Greg finished the year with a record of 19–2 and an ERA of only 1.63. He was the first right-handed pitcher in more than seventy-five years to put together back-to-back seasons with an ERA lower than 2.00. Everyone expected him to win his unprecedented fourth Cy Young Award in a row. When people tried to compare Greg with other pitchers, they had to compare him to those who were already in the Hall of Fame.

But now that the regular season was over, Greg knew none of that mattered. If he didn't lead the Braves to a world championship, the season would be a disappointment.

In the first round of the playoffs, the Braves faced the Colorado Rockies, the surprise winners of the National League West. The hard-hitting Rockies would provide a formidable challenge to Greg and his Atlanta teammates.

Greg looked forward to pitching against the Rockies. He wanted to prove to everyone that his performance during the regular season had been no fluke. Besides, in his previous appearances in the postseason, he hadn't pitched as well as he knew he could. Here was his chance.

Greg pitched the first game in Colorado. After three and a half innings, the Braves led, 1–0.

Although the Rockies hadn't scored yet, Greg was struggling. His control was a little off, and the Rockies were getting their share of base hits. Then, in the fourth, they knocked him around and scored three runs, two on a homer by Vinny Castilla. The Braves scored only once, giving the Rockies a 3–2 lead.

The Braves tied the score in the sixth. Greg left the game after the seventh inning with the score still knotted at 3–3.

Greg had been the Braves' leader all season long. Now, it was his teammates' turn to give him some help. They didn't let him down.

Each team scored a single run in the eighth, so the score was still tied at the beginning of the ninth inning.

Enter Chipper Jones. The Braves rookie hit his second home run of the game to put Atlanta up 5–4. Reliever Mark Wohlers held on to give the Braves the win. Although Greg didn't get the decision, he was happy that the Braves had managed to win the game.

They won again in the ninth inning the next day, scoring four times to come from behind and steal the game 7–4.

But the Rockies refused to give up. They won Game Three in Atlanta, 7–5.

Greg was scheduled to pitch Game Four. If he won, the Braves would win the playoff series.

Again, Greg struggled. In the third inning, he gave up a long home run to Colorado outfielder Dante Bichette. The Rockies led, 3–0.

Once again, Greg's teammates came to his rescue. They pounded five Colorado pitchers for fifteen hits and ten runs. At the day's end, they beat Colorado, 10–4, and earned the right to play the Cincinnati Reds in a best-of-seven-game series for the National League pennant. They were four victories away from the World Series.

But people were starting to talk about the way Greg was pitching. Had he been anyone else, no one would have worried. But he was Greg Maddux. He simply hadn't pitched as well against Colorado as everyone had expected. A few members of the press speculated that Greg couldn't handle the pressure of the postseason.

Then the truth slipped out. It wasn't the pressure that was bothering Greg. It was his arm. After pitching more than two hundred innings in each of the last eight seasons and leading the league in innings pitched for five straight years, his arm was tired. He had a slight case of tendinitis in his pitching shoulder.

But Greg didn't use the injury to make any excuses for his performance, and he didn't complain. The team doctor had told him he could still pitch. Greg wasn't about to allow a tired arm to keep him from his goal.

Fortunately, because of the fact that Greg had pitched the last game against Colorado, he wouldn't be able to start the first or second games of the championship series against Cincinnati. The way the schedule was set up, Greg wouldn't pitch until Game Three, giving him an extra day of rest.

In the meantime, his teammates proved that they could win without him. In Game One, the Braves eked out a last-minute win, beating the Reds 2–1 in eleven innings. They did it again in Game Two, waiting until the tenth inning to score four runs and win, 6–2.

Then came Game Three. Greg's arm felt great. This time, everyone saw the best pitcher in baseball. Greg stayed ahead on just about every hitter. He didn't give up a hit until the third inning.

In the eighth, he finally tired and gave up a run on three straight hits. But the Braves had already scored five runs of their own. Greg turned the game over to the bullpen, and the Braves went on to win, 5–2.

The next game, they swept Greg's favorite childhood team from the playoffs. A 6–0 victory put the National League pennant in the Braves' hands. The Braves were going to the World Series! This time, they planned to win.

That's all Greg Maddux cared about.

Chapter Twelve
1995

Getting the Ring

Greg Maddux was the best pitcher in baseball. The Atlanta Braves were one of the best teams in baseball.

But the Cleveland Indians, champions of the American League, were absolutely awesome.

At almost every position, the Indians had an All-Star. Their pitching staff, the best in the American League, was deep and experienced. Between them, starters Dennis Martinez and Orel Hershiser had won more than 380 games in their careers. Indian relief pitcher Jose Mesa led the big leagues in saves with forty-six.

But as good as their pitching was, their offense was even better. Seven of their starting players hit .300 or better. Outfielder Albert Belle had crushed fifty home runs during the regular season, and four other players had hit more than twenty. Center fielder Kenny Lofton was the best lead-off man in baseball and had stolen fifty-four bases. Designated hitter–first baseman Eddie Murray had collected his three thousandth career base hit earlier in the season and was a certain Hall of Famer. During the regular season, the Indians had fashioned a record of 100–44, one of the best in the history of major league baseball.

In the American League playoffs, Cleveland had easily defeated the Boston Red Sox and the Seattle Mariners. The Indians looked unbeatable.

Everyone expected the series to come down to Cleveland's hitting versus the Braves' starting pitching. Based upon the performance of each team in the playoffs thus far, Cleveland was favored to win.

The series began in Atlanta on Saturday, October 21. Ace pitcher Orel Hershiser started for the Indians. In ten previous postseason appearances over the course of his career, he was undefeated.

Greg Maddux started for the Braves.

Before the series the Indians had studied scouting reports on Greg and watched videotapes of him pitching. What they saw made them feel confident. They thought they could hit any pitcher in base-ball.

But as the Indians would soon find out, Greg Maddux wasn't like any other pitcher in baseball.

At first, it looked as if the Indians were as good as everyone said. In the first inning of Game One, lead-off hitter Kenny Lofton reached base on Braves shortstop Rafael Belliard's error. As Greg struck out the number two hitter, Omar Vizquel, the speedy Lofton stole second and third. With only one out, Lofton was only ninety feet away from giving Cleveland a 1–0 lead.

He traveled that ninety feet when Carlos Baerga grounded out to second base to score an unearned run. Then Greg shut down the dangerous Albert Belle to end the inning. The Indians led, 1–0. Cleveland fans were ready to celebrate.

Then Greg Maddux slammed the door.

Using his dazzling collection of fastballs, curves, change-ups, and cutters, Greg toyed with the vaunted Indians hitters. When they expected the ball outside, he threw inside. When they looked in, he went out. When they looked for the fastball, he threw the change-up. And when they sat back and waited for the change-up, he either threw a curve or blew the fastball right past them.

It wasn't until the fourth inning that the Indians even got the ball out of the infield, when Omar Vizquel flied out. It was the fifth inning before Greg gave up a hit, when Jim Thome singled and was left stranded.

But in the meantime, Orel Hershiser was pitching just as well for Cleveland. Hershiser was one of Greg's favorite pitchers. Like Greg, Hershiser didn't throw very hard. He pitched the way Greg did.

But Hershiser made an early mistake. In the second inning, Fred McGriff homered to tie the score. Then Hershiser stopped the Braves. Entering the seventh inning, the score was tied, 1–1.

In the top of the inning, Greg sent all three Indians batters back to the dugout shaking their heads.

Fred McGriff led off the seventh for Atlanta. Remembering the home run, Hershiser pitched carefully. He walked McGriff. Now he was in real trouble. The winning run was on base. David Justice stepped to the plate. Hershiser tried, but something was wrong. He walked Justice, too.

The Indians' pitching coach raced out to the mound to talk with his pitcher. Hershiser surprised him by telling him he was all through. Relief pitcher Paul Assenmacher entered the game.

Assenmacher was no better than Hershiser. He walked Mike Devereaux to load the bases. Suddenly, the door was open a crack.

The Indians replaced Assenmacher with Julian Tavarez. He got pinch hitter Luis Polonia to hit a ground ball for a force out, but McGriff scored on the play. The Braves led, 2–1.

Then Braves manager Bobby Cox decided to gamble. With light-hitting shortstop Rafael Belliard at bat, he signaled for the "suicide squeeze" play, a bunt. The play is called the "suicide" because if the batter misses the ball, the runner is "dead," a sure out at the plate. The runner at third, Dave Justice, was so surprised he checked with the third base coach to make sure he had read the signal correctly. He had.

As Tavarez wound up, Justice broke for home. Belliard squared around to bunt. Belliard dropped the ball down perfectly. Justice raced across the plate as the Indians threw to first to put out Belliard. The Braves now led, 3–1.

They might as well have led by fifty runs. With a two-run lead and only one inning left to play, Greg Maddux was not going to lose the game.

He set the Indians down in order in the eighth and entered the ninth inning needing only three more outs to get the win.

Paul Sorrento grounded out for out number one. Then Kenny Lofton singled, only the second Cleveland hit of the game.

Braves fans started to squirm in their seats as Cleveland fans started screaming and yelling, but Greg was unconcerned. With a two-run lead, Lofton didn't matter. He concentrated on the hitter.

Omar Vizquel grounded out to second. Lofton advanced on the play, then tried for third.

Fred McGriff threw the ball across the diamond to try to catch the swift Cleveland runner, but he threw the ball away, and Lofton scored.

Now the score was 3–2. There were two outs in the ninth inning. Carlos Baerga was at bat for Cleveland.

Greg threw. Baerga swung.

Bat met ball, and the ball popped high in the air in foul territory along the third base line. Greg watched as it dropped from the night sky. Third baseman Chipper Jones drifted beneath it, then squeezed the ball in his glove.

Out! The Braves, and Greg Maddux, had won.

After the game, everyone agreed that Greg's performance was one of the greatest in World Series history. He gave up only two hits, walked none, and struck out four. Both Cleveland runs were unearned.

"We knew he was good," said Cleveland catcher Sandy Alomar after the game, "but that was ridiculous. That wasn't even fair."

"He is everything you want a pitcher to be," added Cleveland manager Mike Hargrove. "I've been around this game a long time and I've never seen a better performance."

Greg's teammates were just as effusive in their praise. "It was a joke," said fellow starting pitcher Steve Avery. "He showed why he's the best pitcher in the game."

About the only player who didn't have much to

say was Greg. "My guys made the plays behind me," was all he said. "I'm very happy with the game's outcome."

He was very happy, indeed, but he knew the series wasn't over. The Braves still had to win three more games.

The other Braves pitchers had watched Greg closely in Game One. His success with off-speed pitches and control gave them the confidence to use the same strategy.

In Game Two, Tom Glavine used his change-up to confound the powerful Cleveland bats again. The Braves went up, two games to none.

It wasn't until Game Three that the Cleveland offense did much damage. They teed off against John Smoltz and then withstood a Braves comeback to win, 7–6. But in Game Four it was a different story. Unlike Smoltz, who depended on a fastball and a slider, Steve Avery had a change-up, too. He used it to his advantage and beat the Indians, 5–2.

The Braves entered Game Five needing only one win to capture the series. Once again, it was Greg Maddux against Orel Hershiser.

But Greg was still tired after his win in Game

One. All the innings he had thrown were catching up with him. He pitched well, but Hershiser was just a little bit better.

Greg hung on and pitched seven gutsy innings, giving up four runs but keeping the Braves in the game and giving them a chance to win. But this time it was Hershiser who baffled the Atlanta hitters. Cleveland won, 5–4.

The Indians weren't completely free of the greatest pitcher in baseball. Though he wouldn't take the mound in the next game, he could still offer his expertise. Braves pitcher Tom Glavine, scheduled to start Game Six, talked with Greg before the game. He wasn't quite sure how to pitch to the Indians. After seeing them score four runs off Greg in Game Five, he was afraid the Indians were starting to adjust to the steady diet of off-speed pitches they were being served by the Braves staff. He wondered if it was time to start throwing more fastballs.

"Wait a minute," interrupted Greg. "I don't think they're adjusting. I was off a little bit. It wasn't them; it was me. You should just go out and pitch your game. Whatever you do, don't change."

When the best pitcher in baseball tells you not to change, you listen. Glavine did.

He responded with the best game of his career. He pitched even better than Greg had in Game One, giving up only a single hit in eight innings as batter after batter waved feebly at his change-up. Greg was right. They hadn't adjusted.

Dave Justice's sixth-inning home run provided the only run the Braves needed. They defeated the Indians 1–0 to become world champions!

Greg rushed out of the dugout to join his teammates on the field after the game in one big happy pile of Atlanta Braves. He didn't care that he hadn't been on the mound for the final out. He didn't care that he hadn't even gotten to pitch in the game that had won it all. That was fine with him.

All that mattered was that the Braves had won. He knew that when he looked down at his hand, he would soon see something he had waited a long time for.

A ring that said WORLD CHAMPIONS.

For Greg Maddux, the best pitcher in baseball, that said it all.

The #1 Sports Writer for Kids

Read them all!